# MAKING THE GRADE

## FOURTH EDITION

The Aspiring

## Actuary's Guidebook

to Consistent Exam Success and
Advancement in the Workplace

## NICHOLAS MOCCIOLO, FSA, FRM

ACTEX Publications, Inc.
Winsted, Connecticut

Requests for permission should be addressed to
    ACTEX Publications
    P.O. Box 974
    Winsted, CT 06098


Manufactured in the United States of America

10 9 8 7 6 5 4 3 2 1

Cover design by Jeff Melaragno

Library of Congress Cataloging-in-Publication Data

Mocciolo, Nicholas, 1976-
  Making the grade : the aspiring actuary's guidebook to consistent exam
success and advancement in the workplace / Nicholas Mocciolo, FSA,
MAAA. -- Fourth edition.
    pages cm
  Includes bibliographical references and index.
  ISBN 978-1-62542-012-1 (pbk. : alk. paper) 1. Actuaries. 2. Risk
(Insurance) I. Title.
  HG8781.M623 2013
  368'.01076--dc23

                                    2013010039

ISBN: 978-1-62542-012-1

# CONTENTS

## Chapter 4: Written Answer Examinations   55

## Chapter 5: General Preparatory Guidelines   81

# $\mathfrak{F}$OREWORD

Like any highly regarded credentialing process, actuarial exams are just downright hard.

The syllabus materials are long and extremely mathematically intensive. The exams are many, and can take even the brightest candidates 5 to 10 years to complete. The length and uncertainty in completion time can create motivational difficulties, especially for candidates with active family lives and any obligations or interests that extend outside of the workplace. Candidates generally work full-time while studying for exams. While this carries the advantage of current income relative to the credentialing processes of other professions, it leaves little room for recreation and social activities, and may sometimes place pressure on study schedules. The required competencies for future actuaries are growing at an accelerated rate to accommodate the emergence of actuaries into previously unconventional areas of employment. All of these issues, and more, make for a credentialing system that is among the world's most rigorous.

Like that of many professions, the actuarial credentialing process, though arduous, does help to ensure that those who successfully complete it have acquired the requisite proficiencies. In the case of actuaries, this generally translates into mathematical aptitude, a sound work ethic, a problem-solving orientation, and a host of other qualities. This is critical to employers, who rely on the integrity of actuarial designations when making staffing decisions. It is critical for candidates, who rely on the knowledge base and employment leverage gained through the pursuit of professional actuarial credentials for their livelihood. It sustains the prestige, health, and future viability of the actuarial profession and its members. For all of these reasons, and more, it is of paramount importance that the process remains sufficiently rigorous to ensure that the achievement of an actuarial designation provides a concrete demonstration of the acquisition of the necessary skills.

Not surprisingly, I too am interested in preserving the integrity of my actuarial designations. I am reminded of the infamous story of a future Hall-of-Fame Football player who graduated from one of America's finest institutions of higher learning, only to publicly announce years later that he was illiterate. Naturally, the alumni of the institution were outraged; how valuable could their academic credentials be if those not proficient in elementary academic skills could earn them all the same?

However, my interest in ensuring the rigor and professionalism of actuarial credentials is certainly consistent with a desire to help pave the road of passage for the actuaries of tomorrow. I first conceived of this book in a familiar position, during a moment of mental fatigue. There I was, slumped over a desk in the University of Connecticut law library, temporarily straying from the task at hand, dreaming about finishing actuarial exams. I hadn't watched nighttime television or played cards in weeks. I hadn't eaten a square meal in four days, nor had I gone a day without coffee in four months. My eyes burned, I was sleep-deprived, and I was pretty sure that nothing on earth was less important to me at that moment than claim triangles for group disability insurance. I resolved, then and there, to share whatever information I could to help future aspiring actuaries better cope with exams.

I always took notice of the study habits and exam strategies of peers. I frequently dialogued with them during study breaks about their areas of concern, the techniques they found to work for them, and the approaches they would advocate for and against. Gradually, albeit unintentionally, I collected a wealth of information about the actuarial exam processes and the ways in which different people approached them. In addition, I had learned many valuable lessons during my own pursuit of Fellowship, mostly the hard way, and it seemed only right to save others from many of the frustrations and mishaps with which I had been forced to contend.

It is therefore with great pleasure, and great excitement, that I deliver this book to you, the current or future actuarial student. It represents not only the culmination of my own journey through the actuarial credentialing process, but also the collective wisdom of a group of colleagues with whom I have shared many of these experiences. Obviously, there was not uniform consensus regarding every issue and study tactic discussed in this book. However, it was reassuring that despite various points of view with respect to many of the details and nuances of actuarial self-study, the group consistently agreed upon the central tenets of sound exam preparation strategies. This suggests that while each student should formulate the strategy that is most congruent with his or her unique learning style, such a formulation should take place around a predefined "anchor," a set of core competencies for passing actuarial exams that should not be ignored.

My goal in writing this book is to share that anchor with you. And, while most of the book is devoted to anchoring your voyage through actuarial exams, I have also included some general commentary on some other areas of interest to aspiring actuaries. These are a review of the major actuarial organizations in the United States and Canada, a description of the credentialing process of each, and a chapter devoted to issues of skill advancement and professionalism apart from exam success and technical competency. My sincere hope is that these pages make the transition through the actuarial exam process as smooth as possible, and provide you with a set of tips, techniques, and insights that will prove useful for years to come, even in your career after exams.

Undoubtedly, the work required to pass actuarial exams is worth the effort. A career as an actuary has many truly unique characteristics and extraordinary benefits. The job "actuary" has consistently been rated as one of the best jobs in America, according to the *Jobs Rated Almanac*. Actuaries perform a vital function in the ongoing viability of society by modeling and mitigating risk of many different types. The public awareness of actuaries is increasing. The roles of actuaries in the business, governmental, and academic communities are expanding. Actuaries are very well compensated for their work, and most agree that they possess greater than average job security.

But apart from the salary statistics, job growth projections, and other scientific reasons that support the pursuit of an actuarial career, I can honestly say that I love what I do. I am both fulfilled and challenged by my job on an ongoing basis. I am often called upon by company management to solve important problems that are critical to ongoing business growth. I derive a great deal of personal satisfaction from performing a job function that contributes to societal well-being by adding stability to financial security systems and working to ensure that people are protected from life's worst tragedies. In my opinion, passing the actuarial exams while certainly a demanding undertaking is a small price to pay for the countless benefits of a career as an actuary, and I hope that this book helps to get you there.

Feel free to contact me at retail@ActexMadRiver.com should you wish to share any of your feedback regarding this book. I would be very interested in hearing your stories, your opinions, and how this book has impacted you.

I wish you all the best on your exams, in your career, and in your life.


Nicholas P. Mocciolo, FSA
March 2013

# ACKNOWLEDGEMENTS

I'd like to thank Gail Hall at ACTEX for her feedback and constant commitment to this project, now in its fourth edition. In addition, special thanks go to Sandi Lynn for her consistent support and ideas, to Jeff for a fantastic cover design, and to Marilyn for her painstakingly precise typesetting.

I also wish to thank the remaining ACTEX staff for their wonderful support of my initiatives as well as all of the actuarial exam systems. Though it may not be apparent to many, thousands of actuaries worldwide have careers that were made possible by ACTEX and its commitment to the profession.

I would like to thank my children – Alessandro, Eva, and Anya, for playing with me at the beach, doing their chores with pride, covering our walls with their art, celebrating spirit, and making me laugh until it hurts.

Finally, and most importantly, I would like to thank my wife and life partner, Alyssa. Just when I think you are out of surprises, I discover something else to learn from you, to admire about you, or to simply stare in awe of. We found one another, and it was not an accident. I could not have imagined a better life, and it is all because of you. I love you forever.

Nicholas P. Mocciolo, FSA
March 2013

*To my wife, Alyssa, with love,*
*for her unparalleled support of my dreams,*
*her aggressive pursuit of her own,*
*and her unwavering commitment to ours.*

# 1

# $\mathfrak{I}$NTRODUCTION

## 1.1 PURPOSE

There is certainly no shortage of study manuals, textbooks, practice exams, exam-prep seminars, and other resources designed to aid aspiring actuaries in preparing for actuarial exams. All of these products share one common characteristic: they are aimed at enhancing *subject matter expertise*, rather than improving the *methodologies* of preparation and exam-taking. Admittedly, there is the occasional blurb devoted to this topic, such as the <u>Society of Actuaries' Guide to SOA Written Exams</u>, or a publication containing a collection of random study tips from past exam takers. Given the many nuances of actuarial self-study, however, the mixture of technical and non-technical subject matter on the exams, the sheer length of the process, and other intervening variables, these scattered resources are simply not adequate for fully preparing the next generation of actuaries. Furthermore, they are often incomplete or inaccurate, and sometimes contradict one another, making it difficult for aspiring actuaries to derive the intended level of value from them. In short, a comprehensive resource that fully addresses the plethora of issues with which actuarial students must contend remains noticeably absent.

This book aims to fill this void by providing detailed information and recommendations regarding every aspect of the various actuarial credentialing processes from Calculus through Fellowship and beyond. While simply consolidating the information from the isolated, currently available sources might alleviate students of the

1

burden of searching, it would do little to resolve the confusion created by conflicting advice, nor would it lend any credibility to the proposed methods. Thus, I have not aimed to provide a compilation of extraneous pieces of actuarial exam-prep literature (although in some appropriate situations, this is an unintended consequence). Rather, in addition to sharing my own outlook on exam-prep, study techniques, and test-taking skills, I have interwoven the perspectives of members of a select group of actuaries with extraordinary exam and career success who have graciously volunteered to contribute their feedback.

Actuarial credentialing is like no other professional development process; it includes among the longest and most difficult series of credentialing examinations the world over. Their successful completion requires a combination of sound analytical proficiency, good business sense, a strong work ethic, moderate writing skill, an orientation toward detail, and arguably, a little luck. This book seeks to familiarize you with actuarial exams, aid you in your journey through your chosen credentialing process, and provide you with a few words of wisdom for your career after exams.

In the rest of this chapter, I will briefly discuss some of the difficulties you will face in your excursion, but only to better equip you to grapple with these obstacles in a proactive manner. It is not my goal to scare you away from an extremely dynamic and rewarding career as an actuary. In fact, it is my opinion that these potential stumbling blocks are a small price to pay for the opportunity to learn an intricate domain of applied mathematics, to tackle some of the world's most important and complex problems, and to work with bright, motivated people in an active environment, all of which have paid countless dividends in my pursuit of happiness. This has tended to be a popular opinion; **actuary** has consistently been rated in the top 5 jobs in America by the *Jobs Rated Almanac*, and, according to the firm Challenger, Gray, and Christmas, Inc., actuaries are second on the list of hot, high-paying jobs.

## 1.2  CONFOUNDING DIFFICULTIES

Undoubtedly, the number of actuarial exams and the inherent difficulty of their subject matter are sufficient to create an arduous credentialing process for aspiring actuaries. There are, however, multiple other factors that exacerbate this challenge.

First, preparing for an actuarial exam is likely to be very different from preparing for most other exams that you have previously taken, such as final exams in a collegiate setting. Generally speaking, you will devote more cumulative effort to the passage of actuarial exams than to any other examination-related process in your life. There are three obvious consequences of this disparity in the required preparation effort:

- It may be possible that the most efficient and effective manner in which to prepare is not immediately clear. After all, without previously being forced to master such a large amount of material in such a short amount of time, and possibly without the aid of classroom instruction, you may find that your study skills or information retention abilities are in need of improvement;

- You may find that a boost to your will power and a shot to your ego will be necessary to be successful on actuarial exams. Though it is possible that a few college courses may allow you to pass some of the earlier exams without many additional independent study hours, this same pattern will not generally be true for your post-college exams;

- You will be forced to develop, perhaps for the first time in your life, an organizational plan or study schedule that extends for several months. You may not have had opportunities to fully develop time management skills in your previous endeavors, particularly if, as is often the case with intelligent actuarial students, you were able to succeed in college with negligible planning.

Second, the more time passes, the more difficult it is to complete actuarial exams. For many candidates, with each passing year, other responsibilities, such as family, community, and workplace obligations, begin to overshadow the importance of exams, making it progressively harder for them to justify time spent studying. This is especially true for exam candidates with children.

Third, the length of time necessary for completion of exams is significant, creating possible motivational barriers. While exceptions certainly exist, those who attain Fellowship in a professional actuarial society have tended to do so in five to ten years. This has proven to be a major deterrent for some candidates, since it subtly obscures the connection between their daily study activities and their long-term professional goals. This issue has been somewhat mitigated by recent changes in the educational systems of several major actuarial organizations, with the hope of reducing "travel time" and/or increasing its predictability. The time commitment, however, remains substantial.

Fourth, the actuarial profession is one of the few whose students are forced to simultaneously work full-time and self-educate for the duration of their credentialing processes. This quasi-apprenticeship approach is unlike that of medicine, law, or most other white-collar disciplines, in which candidates graduate from professional school and begin their practicing careers only upon attainment of the terminal credential in their respective fields. This is not to ignore the typical internship, practicum, or rotation commonly completed by individuals in these other professions, but only to say that the proportion of time spent doing both activities simultaneously is less. While this arrangement has definite advantages (it enables you to begin earning a relatively significant income far earlier in your career, and reduces the need for student loans), it can sometimes create stress in balancing your work, study, and home lives.

I have undoubtedly omitted other significant obstacles in your quest for Fellowship in a professional actuarial society. Indeed, there are many macro-level dynamics that impede rapid progression through the exams, as well as many unique, personal challenges that must be overcome by each individual. It suffices to say that aspiring actuaries face a double-edged sword; examinations of an inherently challenging nature, further complicated by the presence of many additional barriers to success that are not present in competing disciplines.

## 1.3 FIGHTING BACK

Despite the rigor of exams and the numerous confounding factors described earlier, there are many individuals who have completed exams in a relatively short amount of time. While some would be tempted to casually attribute the widely varying rate of success on actuarial exams purely to intellect or analytical capacity, this would be a gross oversimplification. Undoubtedly, for at least one course in your educational career, you had an instructor whose teaching methods simply did not mesh with your learning style. As a result, you either expended undue effort to learn the material in accordance with your personal standards, or you moved through the course while earning less than your typical grade. You can therefore attest that the teaching and learning techniques employed are just as explanatory of the classroom results as the people trying to learn. It is certainly a reasonable inference that this relationship also holds for the nuances of actuarial self-study. As a result, focusing your energy on the *method of preparation* as well as the subject matter can significantly impact your record of success on exams.

My goal in writing this text is to present both general and specific advice on study and exam strategies that will help make your transition through exams as smooth as possible. For credibility, I have listed my personal exam record in Table 1.1.

The numbering systems in place when I took the exams were totally different from the current system, which began in 2007. Consequently the exam names used in Table 1.1 are not likely to be meaningful to you. Note that I did not sit for an exam during the Fall 2000 exam period, since I wanted to enjoy my last semester of college without the burden of exams looming over my head!

**TABLE 1.1**

| Sitting | Exam(s) | Score(s) |
|---|---|---|
| Spring 1999 | 100 | 9 |
| Fall 1999 | 110, 140 | 10, 7 |
| Spring 2000 | 3 | 8 |
| Fall 2000 | None | N/A |
| Spring 2001 | 4 | 8 |
| Fall 2001 | 5 | 9 |
| Spring 2002 | 6 | 10 |
| Fall 2002 | 8V | 10 |
| 2003 | 7 Pre-test | Pass |
| 2003 | 7 Seminar | Pass |
| 2004 | PD | Pass |
| 2004 | FAC | Attain FSA |

My record indicates that success on the first attempt on every exam is attainable. While this is certainly my hope for each of you reading this book, the strategies and techniques presented here will aid in your success even if they do not grant you invulnerability to failure. It is a commonly held view, however, that a universally correct or optimal study methodology does not exist. I will, therefore, avoid making recommendations that worked for me *merely because they worked for me*, and instead, focus on presenting preparation and exam-taking techniques that have proven successful for a cross-section of very exam-adept actuaries. Not surprisingly, their views tend to corroborate my personal beliefs within a range that is narrow enough to suggest general themes but wide enough to maintain the integrity of individual educational variation. The integration of our collective ideologies – a comprehensive set of strategies, guidelines, techniques, and tips that has produced reliably sound exam outcomes – is what lies ahead of you in this book. The hope, of course, is that it proves effective for you.

Critics have always been skeptical about the merits of such discussion, asserting that the one and only way to bolster your chance of success on an actuarial exam is to study harder. These are generally the same individuals who pompously declare that failure despite sufficient study time is indicative of a lack of intelligence or analytical competence. While it is certainly feasible that a student may fail repeatedly due to insufficient aptitude, such broad-based criticisms exaggerate this possibility to ludicrous proportions. While it is a point of fact that extremely intelligent students may be able to get away with less work, this hardly implies that scrutiny of exam preparation strategies is useless, nor does it negate the potential impact of a concentrated effort to hone study skills. Many very intelligent, properly motivated actuarial students fail exams; this reality alone ought to be sufficient to demonstrate that proper study methods are crucial. The fact that they are taken for granted does not invalidate their significance.

In this text, I will present recommendations in a logical, organized way. I begin in Chapter 2 by providing an overview of the actuarial profession, the major actuarial organizations in the U.S. and Canada, and a brief synopsis of the current education systems of the Society of Actuaries, the Casualty Actuarial Society, the Joint Board for Enrollment of Actuaries, and the Canadian Institute of Actuaries. In Chapter 3, I discuss the preliminary actuarial examinations, including strategies and tactics aimed specifically at preparation for these exams. In Chapter 4, I provide similar coverage of upper level exams. In Chapter 5, I review some general preparation and exam-taking suggestions that are applicable to all actuarial exams, including the attitudinal dynamics of studying, the construction of study schedules, and even the power of superstition. The book concludes with Chapter 6, in which I focus on additional competencies, apart from mastery of the exam subject matter, that you will need in order to achieve career success as an actuary. After all, exams are tough, but they are only part of the overall picture.

## 1.4  A NOTE ON WELL-ROUNDEDNESS

While reading this book, I encourage you, at the risk of gratuitously imposing a personal value, to be cognizant of one fundamental ideal. Exams, no matter how important they may seem, or how much of a challenge they represent, should not be pursued at the expense of your emotional, physical, or spiritual health. I am not addressing a few all-night study binges, skipped meals, or mild fits of anxiety, all of which are generally regarded as natural expectations in the demanding pursuit of achievement. Rather, I am referring to a few occasional and unfortunate events I have witnessed during my career in which people's lives have truly been damaged in a long-lasting way due to their approach to exams. Keeping exams in perspective, and regarding them as an important and worthwhile goal but not a survival necessity, will help to ensure your health. No person should spend five to ten years as a miserable "exam machine" with deteriorating health and eroding personal relationships due to the over-prioritization of actuarial exams. No person should be afflicted with prolonged insomnia, depression, or a weakened state of health due to self-imposed exam pressure. Finally, no person should pursue exams with such passion that the cultivation of prosperity in other areas of life is precluded. After all, exams are exams – no more, and no less.

# 2

# THE ACTUARIAL PROFESSION AND ITS EDUCATION SYSTEMS

## 2.1 INTRODUCTION

Prior to covering the mechanics of studying for and taking actuarial exams, I thought it would be very beneficial to provide a high-level overview of the actuarial profession. In particular, I will begin by briefly describing what actuaries are and the type of work they do. I will then discuss the major actuarial organizations in the United States and Canada, and the various membership statuses they bestow. Finally, I will detail some of the systems through which actuaries are credentialed.

Most of the discussion in this chapter, particularly that pertaining to actuarial work and organizations, will be broad. The wide variety of actuarial specialties and the many nuances of the numerous actuarial organizations and exam systems in the world make a fully detailed synopsis of these topics beyond the scope of this text. My goal is to present you with general descriptions, and enable you to make the distinctions between major areas of practice and the prominent actuarial organizations in the U.S. and Canada. Should you desire more detailed information about any of the organizations or exam systems discussed here, I encourage you to do additional research. To that end, I have concluded the chapter with a comprehensive set of educational resources for your reference.

## 2.2 WHAT IS AN ACTUARY?

Risk is all around you. It is easy to envision some of the events that might cause you to incur an unexpected financial loss. Consider the potential impact of the untimely death of the primary wage earner of your household. Suppose a flood or fire was to destroy your home. Perhaps you or a loved one suffered an accident or contracted an illness that required expensive medical treatment. Indeed, there are many uncertainties in life against which you require protection, since the consequences could be devastating.

The endeavors of many public and private organizations also entail significant financial risks. Pension plans, both public and private, are obligated to pay benefits to retirees, and run the risk that future funds will not be sufficient. Corporations and governmental agencies construct office buildings and factories, and run the risk that they will be destroyed by a natural disaster. Banks commit to paying accountholders interest on CDs and savings accounts, and run the risk that they will have insufficient funds.

As individuals, we generally rid ourselves of the most significant risks by purchasing insurance; while the risk may thus be eliminated from our own lives, it does not disappear altogether. Rather, the risk is transferred to the insurance company, where it must be managed. Organizations may also choose to transfer their risks to insurers or to other establishments. They may also choose to manage them internally.

Risk is not necessarily a bad thing; in many cases, considerable financial rewards are available to institutions that can properly measure and manage it. This, however, can be very challenging. In many cases, it is unclear how often financial losses will arise, and if they do arise, how significant they will be. Each type of risk has its own unique characteristics, and therefore requires analysis of different factors for it to be properly assessed and managed. Nobody can, for example, be quite sure when the next house will catch fire, and when it does, how significant the damage will be. The likelihood of a house catching fire may depend on many dynamics, including the climate, humidity, living habits of the house's occupants, the style in which the house was constructed, the frequency of arson in a given neighborhood, and others. The amount of damage to the house in the event of a fire will also depend on many factors – the materials used to construct the house, the presence and functionality of smoke detectors and alarm systems, the proximity of the house to a fire station and hydrant, and a host of others.

**Actuaries** are the world's leading professionals in the identification, quantification, and management of financial risk. To properly perform their duties, actuaries draw upon a broad collection of skills. Principally, they must possess sharp analytical minds and a mastery of advanced mathematics. They must also employ leadership abilities, business and organizational knowledge, and a sound understanding of social systems and behavior.

The majority of actuaries have traditionally worked in the insurance industry. While insurers remain the largest employers of actuaries today, the role of the modern-day actuary is steadily evolving. As the risks faced by other industries continue to grow, and the potential for catastrophic loss becomes more prominent, actuaries are being employed by commercial and investment banks, consulting firms, pension plans, and governmental agencies, all with increasing regularity.

Although imperceptible to many individuals, actuaries perform a vital function in society by ensuring the sustainability of public and private financial systems and allowing most of us to live in emotional comfort, knowing that we are largely protected from the financial effects of life's worst tragedies. Many actuaries therefore enjoy tremendous intellectual stimulation and personal satisfaction from their work.

## 2.3 MAJOR ACTUARIAL ORGANIZATIONS IN THE U.S. AND CANADA

### 2.3.1 The Society of Actuaries (SOA)

The **SOA** is a nonprofit organization dedicated to advancing the discipline of actuarial science and bolstering the ability of actuaries to solve problems involving future risk and uncertainty. The SOA is primarily responsible for delivering education to aspiring actuaries (accomplished largely through the administration of exams and online education), promoting and funding research in the field of actuarial science, providing continuing education opportunities to existing members, and interfacing with the higher education community and other professional organizations to facilitate the advancement and expansion of the actuarial profession.

The SOA examination process and ongoing educational and research initiatives are appropriate for most actuaries, and in particular, those wishing to specialize in individual life insurance and annuities, and the related disciplines of group life and health insurance, finance and investments, enterprise risk management, and retirement benefits. Notable exceptions historically were those actuaries intending to practice in the property and casualty insurance industry, though the SOA has recently introduced a Fellowship specialty track related to this segment of the industry for those so inclined.

The SOA currently has more than 22,000 members. Membership in the SOA can be achieved by attaining one of its designations, Associate (**ASA**), Chartered Enterprise Risk Analyst (**CERA**), or Fellow (**FSA**). The specific requirements for attaining these designations will be more thoroughly addressed in section 2.4.1.

The SOA also co-sponsors the enrolled actuaries examinations, leading to the enrolled actuary (EA) designation, which will be more thoroughly described in section 2.4.3.

### 2.3.2 The Casualty Actuarial Society (CAS)
The **CAS** is comparable to the SOA, with the main distinction being its advancement of the field of actuarial science as it pertains specifically to property and casualty (**P&C**) risk exposures. As is the case with the SOA, the CAS delivers education to aspiring actuaries, sponsors professional seminars and workshops, and supports research.

The CAS currently has more than 5,000 members. Membership in the CAS can be achieved by attaining one of its three designations,

Associate (**ACAS**), Chartered Enterprise Risk Analyst (**CERA**) or Fellow (**FCAS**). The CAS also bestows an alternate membership designation, Affiliate, to certain qualified individuals working in the insurance industry who have not earned the ACAS or FCAS designations. The specific requirements for attaining these designations will be more thoroughly addressed in section 2.4.2.

### 2.3.3 The American Academy of Actuaries (AAA)

The **AAA** serves to integrate actuaries from all practice areas, and represent the actuarial community in the United States with respect to issues of public interest and professionalism. The mission of the AAA is to serve the public and the United States actuarial profession. In doing so, the AAA performs, among others, the following critical functions for the profession:

1. It creates and upholds actuarial standards of ethical conduct and practice, and resolves questions, complaints, and inquiries regarding the same through its Actuarial Board for Counseling and Discipline (**ABCD**);

2. It represents the actuarial profession to the public;

3. It assists relevant political and legislative initiatives by providing actuarial analysis;

4. It provides opportunities for professional development of its members through volunteerism and service to the profession;

5. It works to bolster the public's understanding of the role and importance of actuaries in society.

The vision of the AAA is that financial security systems in the United States be sound and sustainable, and that actuaries be the preeminent experts in risk and financial security. Membership in the AAA is denoted by the designation **MAAA**, and may be granted to those with three years of professional actuarial experience that have earned Associateship or Fellowship in the SOA or CAS, or who meet membership requirements from certain other professional actuarial organizations. The AAA currently has approximately 17,000 members.

### 2.3.4 The American Society of Pension Professionals and Actuaries (ASPPA)

**ASPPA** is a professional organization aimed at educating pension actuaries, consultants, and pension plan administrators, and to support the ongoing viability of a national retirement income policy.

There are many different designations offered by ASPPA. The membership categories are split into four distinct tracks, supporting seven different credentials, as follows:

1. The Plan Administration, Compliance, and Consulting Track can lead to the Qualified 401(k) Administrator (**QKA**), Qualified Pension Administrator (**QPA**), or Certified Pension Consultant (**CPC**) designations;

2. The Financial Consulting Track can lead to the Qualified Plan Financial Consultant (**QPFC**) designation;

3. The Tax-Exempt & Governmental Plan Administration, Compliance, and Consulting Track can lead to the Tax-Exempt and Governmental Plan Consultant (**TGPC**) designation;

4. The Actuarial Consulting Track can lead to the Member, Society of Pension Actuaries (**MSPA**) and Fellow, Society of Pension Actuaries (**FSPA**) designations.

Associated professionals are those individuals working in the retirement systems field that possess credentials in alternative disciplines, such as law or accounting. Such individuals with a minimum of three years experience in retirement-plan-related matters may apply for the Associated Professional Member (**APM**) designation.

The one other path to membership is through an affiliation. **Affiliates** are individuals who have an interest in the pension field, and who wish to enjoy the benefits of ASPPA membership, but who have not completed examinations. Affiliates are the only members who lack voting privileges.

ASPPA also co-sponsors the enrolled actuaries examinations, which lead to the enrolled actuary (**EA**) designation, more thoroughly described in section 2.4.3. ASPPA currently has over 10,000 members.

## 2.3.5 The Joint Board for the Enrollment of Actuaries (JBEA)

The Employee Retirement Income Security Act (ERISA) of 1974 was a major legislative initiative that defined a significant portion of current-day pension plan regulations in the United States. The **Joint Board** was established pursuant to section 3041 of ERISA, and is responsible for credentialing individuals wishing to perform actuarial services under ERISA.

The Joint Board, the SOA, and the ASPPA co-sponsor the enrolled actuary examinations, which must be completed in order to earn the enrolled actuary (**EA**) designation. **Enrolled Actuaries** are eligible to perform valuations of qualified pension plans. The specifics of the EA examinations will be covered more extensively in section 2.4.3.

The Joint Board consists of six members, three of whom are appointed by the Secretary of the Treasury, two by the Secretary of Labor, and the last, a nonvoting member, by the Pension Benefit Guaranty Corporation (**PBGC**), a U.S. government agency that insures pension plans.

## 2.3.6 The Canadian Institute of Actuaries (CIA)

The **CIA** is the primary membership organization for actuaries practicing in Canada. Most provincial and federal regulations in Canada maintain that individuals performing actuarial functions required for regulatory compliance must have earned the designation of Fellow (**FCIA**). The CIA is organized to:

1. Promote the advancement of actuarial science through research;

2. Sponsor programs for the education and qualification of members and prospective members;

3. Ensure that actuarial services provided by its members meet extremely high professional standards;

4. Regulate the professional conduct of its membership;

5. Advocate for the profession with governments and the public in the development of public policy.

Its roles are very similar to those of the American Academy of Actuaries in the U. S.

To earn Fellowship in the CIA, candidates must first earn Fellowship in another recognized actuarial organization. Some examples are the SOA, CAS, and many of their foreign counterparts. Most must also successfully complete the CIA's Practice Education Course (**PEC**), and must meet a certain minimum requirement for experience as a practicing actuary both overall and specifically in Canada.

Recently, the CIA modified the requirements for its Associate (**ACIA**) designation to make them more consistent with those of the SOA and CAS. Individuals earning the ASA, ACAS, or CERA designations from the SOA or CAS may qualify to become Associates of the CIA and may use the designation ACIA. Only individuals having earned Fellowship status in the CIA may call themselves actuaries.

The CIA also bestows two alternative member statuses, **Correspondent** and **Affiliate**.

### 2.3.7 The International Actuarial Association (IAA)
The IAA is a worldwide organization of over 80 professional actuarial associations, serving to link together the global actuarial communities and profession. The mission of the IAA is to:

1. Represent the actuarial profession and promote its role, reputation and recognition in the international domain;

2. Promote professionalism, develop education standards and encourage research, with the active involvement of its Member Associations and Sections, in order to address changing needs.

One key philosophical belief of the IAA is that substantial commonalities in the various education systems employed by major actuarial organizations throughout the world will tend to improve the international portability of actuaries and the international recognition of the actuarial profession. To that end, the IAA has published its 2013 IAA Education Guidelines, which contain a summary of "best practices" for actuarial education systems. Actuarial associations wishing to maintain or achieve full membership status in the IAA should have education systems and processes that are consistent with those described in the Guidelines, which address the scope and breadth of desirable education requirements, both technical and non-technical, without being prescriptive.

One important implication of the Guidelines is that they may be particularly valuable in the context of cross recognition of qualifications between various worldwide actuarial organizations. If actuaries are eligible for membership and/or credentialing in various global actuarial organizations by virtue of achieving a designation in one organization, rather than having to complete additional examinations and requirements, then their individual mobility and career portability, as well as the global perception and effectiveness of the profession, should be enhanced. A variety of cross recognition criteria for actuarial designations and membership have already been established, particularly as they pertain to credentials earned from the major actuarial organizations globally, including the SOA and CAS.

### 2.3.8 Other Organizations
There are other actuarial organizations in the U.S. and Canada, as well as internationally, each with a unique mission and profile. A list of some of these organizations, as well as a brief description of each, is provided in section 2.6.

## 2.4 ACTUARIAL EDUCATION SYSTEMS

### 2.4.1 The Society of Actuaries
The current SOA credentialing system was phased in beginning in 2005, and was fully in place by 2007. It is made up of the following four components: prerequisites (including VEE), the preliminary exams (PE), the fundamentals of actuarial practice course (FAP), and the fellowship requirements. Some smaller changes have been implemented since 2007, including the introduction of the CERA designation and its requirements, as well as changes to the fellowship requirements. More information is available on the SOA website at www.soa.org.

### 2.4.1.1 Prerequisites

Under the current exam system, several disciplines are considered prerequisites to pursuing actuarial education. These include calculus, introductory business law, accounting, linear algebra, and basic statistics. There is no formal examination or validation of these topics, but knowledge of them will be intrinsically required in order to pass the formal examinations.

In addition, a candidate is required to learn finance, economics, and applied statistics, and to demonstrate sufficient knowledge of these subjects by earning a grade of B– or higher in an appropriate course at an accredited college or university (or other suitable educational experience as approved by the Society of Actuaries). No SOA-sponsored examination will be required for these topics. This concept is referred to as validation by educational experience (**VEE**).

### 2.4.1.2 The Preliminary Examinations

There are five preliminary exams in the 2007 system:

- *Exam P: Probability*

  This computer-based exam is three hours in length and tests the fundamentals of probability. Although not directly tested, significant proficiency in calculus will be required to complete the exam due to its wide applicability to solving problems pertaining to probability. Note that the passage of this exam will also give credit for CAS Exam 1.

- *Exam FM: Financial Mathematics*

  This exam is three hours in length and covers traditional interest theory as well as an introduction to financial economics. Note that passage of this exam will also give credit for CAS Exam 2.

- *Exam MLC: Actuarial Models – Life Contingencies Segment*

  This exam is three hours in length and tests traditional life contingencies, including single-life, multiple-life, and multiple decrement models. Candidates having successfully completed this exam will receive credit for CAS Exam 3L.

- *Exam MFE*: *Actuarial Models – Financial Economics Segment*

  This three hour exam covers basic aspects of financial economics, including derivative securities and option pricing. Note that passage of this exam will also give credit for CAS Exam 3F.

- *Exam C*: *Construction and Evaluation of Actuarial Models*

  This exam is three and a half hours in length and covers severity, frequency and aggregate models, estimation of model parameters, credibility, and simulation. Note that passage of this exam will also give credit for CAS Exam 4.

### 2.4.1.3 The Fundamentals of Actuarial Practice Course

To attain the ASA designation, one would be required to complete the satisfactory coursework in finance, economics, and applied statistics (VEE), pass each of the five exams described above, and successfully complete both the Associateship Professionalism (**APC**) Course and the Fundamentals of Actuarial Practice (**FAP**) Course. The APC is one-half day in length, and covers professionalism, ethics and legal liability and makes extensive use of the case study method. The FAP is an online course consisting of eight modules, as follows:

- *Role of the Professional Actuary* – Introduce the concept of the control cycle and provide the basic framework for actuarial work;

- *Core External Forces* – Provide an overview of outside influences that impact the work of actuaries;

- *Risk in Actuarial Problems* – A survey of common actuarial problems in traditional financial systems;

- *Actuarial Solutions* – Demonstrate the application of the control cycle approach introduced earlier to the resolution of selected problems;

- *Design and Pricing of an Actuarial Solution* – Introduce and define common models for each practice area;

- *Model Selection and Solution Design* – An overview of the model selection and design process;

- *Selection of Initial Assumptions* – An introduction to setting assumptions and examining model output for reasonableness;

- *Monitoring Results* – An overview of the process for monitoring experience and results.

You will be required to complete exercises throughout the FAP course to demonstrate progression; this will include two comprehensive written assessments.

### 2.4.1.4 CERA

In 2007, the Society of Actuaries introduced an alternative route to the ASA designation. Named the Chartered Enterprise Risk Analyst (or **CERA**), the educational requirements focus on those necessary to succeed in the emerging field of enterprise risk management.

Since that time, the IAA has sponsored an initiative targeted at globalizing the CERA credential. This initiative was brought to a successful conclusion in 2009 through the enactment of the CERA Treaty, a multilateral agreement formalizing a collaboration of the international actuarial profession. The treaty effectively forms a new organization, the CERA Global Association, with the overall mandate of holding and awarding the credential. The Association credentials certain individual actuarial organizations as permissible grantors of the CERA designation based upon universally agreed criteria. At present, there are 14 associations certified to issue the CERA credential, including the SOA.

The SOA made several modifications to its CERA requirements as a result of the treaty. Candidates can now earn the CERA credential through the SOA by completing the following requirements:

1. Satisfactory completion of Exams P, FM, MFE, and C;

2. An acceptable VEE for Economics and Corporate Finance;

3. Satisfactory completion of a targeted 4-hour ERM examination and a new ERM eLearning module, which replaces the operational risk module required in prior years;

4. Completion of the FAP as described in section 2.4.1.3;

5. Completion of the Associateship Professionalism Course (APC).

### 2.4.1.5  The Fellowship Requirements

The Fellowship requirements are also undergoing changes in 2013. To begin the journey to the FSA designation, candidates must declare one of six specialty tracks, representing the subject matter to which their Fellowship education will be devoted. The six tracks are as follows:

1. Group and Health;

2. Individual Life and Annuities;

3. Retirement Benefits;

4. Corporate Finance and Enterprise Risk Management;

5. Quantitative Finance and Investments;

6. General Insurance, which is a new track beginning in 2013, and is focused on traditional insurance applications including property and casualty.

To attain the FSA designation, candidates must earn the ASA credential and complete several additional track-specific requirements. As a general guide, most tracks will require 12 hours of examinations, three eLearning modules, the Decision Making and Communication Module (**DMAC**), and the Fellowship Admissions Course (**FAC**).

2013 also brings some changes to the Fellowship examinations. Beginning in the fall, the exams will change from two 6-hour examinations to two 5-hour (Core and Advanced) examinations and one 2-hour (Fellowship Non-Core) examination.

Another unique aspect of the 2013 structure, which is a result of the focus being placed on the CERA credential and its recent globalization, is that irrespective of a candidate's chosen specialty track, he or she has the option to take the ERM exam in lieu of the 2-hour Fellowship Non-Core exam (the so-called "CERA Option"). While this adds two hours of examination time, it allows for interested candidates of all tracks to receive both the CERA and FSA designations more efficiently than in the past. Note that for the Corporate Finance and Enterprise Risk Management track, the CERA Option is mandatory.

Regarding track-specific modifications, neither the Group and Health nor Individual Life and Annuities tracks will see material changes under the 2013 redesign. In addition, the Retirement Benefits track will remain mostly the same, except that U.S. practitioners now must complete the two EA-2 exams (documented in Section 2.4.3).

Other tracks will undergo more significant changes. Previously, the Advanced Finance / ERM and Advanced Portfolio Management tracks shared the Financial Economic Theory and Engineering (FETE) exam. Beginning in 2013, however, these tracks as redefined will no longer share an examination. The Corporate Finance and Enterprise Risk Management track will provide corporate finance and risk management foundations and education to those aspiring to careers in finance and risk management. The Quantitative Finance and Investments track will focus on investments, hedging, and portfolio management topics for those aspiring to careers in investment management.

The eLearning modules are similar in form to those used in the FAP. They are designed to integrate the topics covered on the Fellowship examinations, and to illuminate the link between these concepts and effective actuarial practice. Each track will require three specific eLearning modules tailored to its educational goals, though some overlap between tracks is possible.

The DMAC focuses on written and oral communication skills and decision–making skills as applied to solving business problems. This module is available to candidates after the completion of all other fellowship requirements *except* the Fellowship Admissions Course.

The FAC is a three-day course focusing on development of selected business, problem-solving, and communication skills and on the potential ethical dilemmas faced by practicing actuaries. In addition, all attendees will be required to complete a short oral presentation. This is the final step toward the achievement of the FSA designation.

Please consult the SOA website for more information on current requirements for each of its three credentials as well as anticipated changes to the education system.

### 2.1.4.6   Education Section of SOA.org

The SOA's website is updated several months prior to each exam's administration. It is an excellent resource for actuarial students, providing the following:

1. The SOA's Pathway to Membership;

2. A list of the examinations to be offered during the next exam period, including the date and time of each exam, a detailed description of each exam's learning objectives and the topics covered, and a list of the required readings for each, if applicable;

3. A complete list of all rules and regulations associated with examinations, including registration deadlines, procedures and forms, permissible writing utensils and calculators, allowable food and beverage items, disciplinary actions for dishonest candidates, a complete list of examination centers, and all other nuances related to examination logistics;

4. A description of the processes used to identify the syllabus, develop and grade exams, and determine the pass mark;

5. A set of suggestions for exam candidates, including study techniques and recommended approaches to various types of examination questions;

6. A list of textbook vendors and publishers and other valuable resources; and

7. Transcripts and historical exam questions and results.

I highly encourage all students to read this section of the SOA website at least once thoroughly and check it again prior to each exam sitting to ensure compliance with any new rules and to maintain awareness of any changes in policy, particularly those related to exam registration, permissible calculators, and the policy on guessing.

### 2.4.1.7    The Grading System

All of the SOA actuarial exams are graded on a scale from 0 to 10. Scores of 6 and above are passing scores, while scores of 5 and below indicate that a candidate has failed. Total exam performance is compared to the official pass mark, and the score is assigned according to the increment (in tenths) within which performance falls. So, for example, if the sum of the points earned on the exam were between 100% and 110% of the passing mark, a candidate would receive a score of 6. Similarly, a score of 9 would indicate that a candidate earned between 130% and 140% of the passing mark, while a score of 0 indicates that a candidate earned less than 50% of the passing mark. Other than providing information about overall performance and signifying whether a candidate has passed or failed, a particular score has no official relevance; that is, a score of 6 has the same official meaning as a score of 9.

For certain examinations, an analysis of results is automatically sent to failing candidates. In the event that a candidate fails an exam and believes that his or her exam was unfairly or improperly graded, a request to have the examination graded again may be submitted. More details on this process are available on the website or by contacting the SOA.

## 2.4.2    The Casualty Actuarial Society

Like the SOA, the CAS also recently changed its system of exams, beginning in 2005 and extending through 2011. The current system includes the following four components: prerequisites (including VEE), online courses, the preliminary exams (PE), and the fellowship requirements. (Each component is described in its own subsection below.) More information on the current system is available on the CAS website at www.casact.org.

### 2.4.2.1    Prerequisites

CAS has the same VEE requirement as does SOA, which is described in the second paragraph of Section 2.4.1.1.

### 2.4.2.2    CAS Online Courses

CAS requires candidates to complete two online courses, each of which prepares them for a two-hour multiple choice exam on its content.

The first, "Risk Management and Insurance Operations", can be waived only for those individuals having earned the Chartered Property Casualty Underwriter (**CPCU**) designation. It covers topics such as risk management and control, risk financing, ERM, insurance operations / marketing / distribution, underwriting, claims, reinsurance, and data management.

The second, "Insurance Accounting, Coverage Analysis, Insurance Law, and Insurance Regulation", cannot be waived. It covers topics such as insurance accounting, policy concepts, personal lines, commercial lines, liability, miscellaneous coverage, and insurance law and regulation.

### 2.4.2.3  Preliminary Examinations
CAS has seven preliminary examinations, as follows:

- *Exam 1*: *Probability*

  Up until the end of 2013, this exam was jointly sponsored by SOA and CAS. Beginning in 2014, CAS will give credit for Exam 1 with successful completion of comparable exams offered by a number of other credentialing organizations.

- *Exam 2*: *Financial Mathematics*

  Credit for this previously co-sponsored exam will be given for successful completion of comparable exams offered by a number of other credentialing organizations.

- *Exam 3F*: *Models for Financial Economics*

  Credit for this previously co-sponsored exam will be given for successful completion of comparable exams offered by a number of other credentialing organizations.

- *Exam 3L*: *Models for Life Contingencies and Statistics*

  This is a two-and-a half-hour exam providing coverage of basic life contingencies, but not to the same extent as SOA Exam MLC. In addition, CAS Exam 3L includes formal examination of mathematical statistics (which SOA treats as a prerequisite topic). Exam 3L is given in both the Spring and Fall. Candidates having passed SOA Exam MLC will receive credit for Exam 3L (though the converse is not true).

Beginning in 2014, Exam 3L will be replaced by two exams:
o Exam 3LC, covering the topics of life contingencies and survival models. Credit for this exam can also be obtained by successful completion of SOA Exam MLC.

o Exam 3ST, covering the topics of statistics and stochastic modeling. At press time, no comparable exams had been identified in other credentialing organizations.

- *Exam 4: Construction and Evaluation of Actuarial Models*

Credit for this previously co-sponsored exam will be given for successful completion of comparable exams offered by a number of other credentialing organizations.

- *Exam 5: Basic Techniques for Ratemaking and Estimating Claim Liabilities*

This is a four-hour exam and generally contains written answer questions. It is offered twice per year in the fall and the spring. It tests knowledge of basic principles underlying P&C insurance, including operational aspects, various lines of business, ratemaking, and classification analysis.

- *Exam 6: Reserving, Insurance Accounting Principles, Reinsurance, and Enterprise Risk Management*

This is a four-hour exam and generally contains written answer questions. It is currently offered in the fall only, but will be offered in both the spring and fall beginning in 2014. The exam is nation-specific, meaning that it is given in three separate forms, one for the U.S., one for Canada, and one for Chinese Taipei. Candidates should choose the examination corresponding to their intended region of practice. It tests knowledge of some insurance law, regulatory constraints on insurers, public and private insurance programs, and financial reporting and taxation.

The ACAS designation is earned by successfully completing the prerequisites (VEE), the two online courses, the seven preliminary examinations, and the CAS Course on Professionalism, a two-day workshop on issues of professionalism and ethics.

### *2.4.2.4 Fellowship Examinations*
In addition to the ACAS requirements, candidates must successfully complete Exams 7, 8, and 9, described below, to earn the FCAS designation.

- *Exam 7 – Estimation of Policy Liabilities, Insurance Company Valuation, and Enterprise Risk Management*

  This is a four-hour exam and generally contains written answer questions. It is offered in the spring only. It tests knowledge of claim estimation and reserving, P&C company valuation, and quantitative evaluation and management of insurance and financial risk.

- *Exam 8 – Advanced Ratemaking*

  This is a four-hour exam and generally contains written answer questions. It is offered in the fall only. It tests knowledge of ratemaking classifications, excess and deductible ratings, catastrophic events, risk loads and contingency provisions, and individual risk rating.

- *Exam 9 – Financial Risk and Rate of Return*

  This is a four-hour exam and generally contains written answer questions. It is offered in the Spring only. It tests knowledge of portfolio theory, ALM, credit risk, liquidity risk, economic capital, risk loads and contingency provisions.

### *2.4.2.5 CERA*
Like SOA, CAS is also certified to issue the CERA designation. To attain a CERA from CAS, candidates must:

- earn the ACAS designation;
- successfully complete CAS exams 7 and 9;

- successfully complete the three-day Enterprise Risk Management and Modeling Seminar for CERA Qualification;

- successfully complete Exam ST9, Enterprise Risk Management Specialist Technical, of the Institute and Faculty of Actuaries (U.K.).

### 2.4.2.6  Policy on Guessing

One important item of note is that the CAS policy regarding guessing on multiple choice questions differs from that of the SOA for some exams. As Exams 1, 2, 3F, and 4 are currently co-sponsored, these examinations have the same policy as that of the SOA (currently no penalty for guessing). This means that candidates maximize their scores on these exams by answering every question. This is also true of CAS online courses 1 and 2. Exam 3L and Exams 5-9, however, are graded such that one-quarter of the point value of each multiple choice question will be deducted in the event you answer it incorrectly. This should make you (statistically) indifferent to guessing randomly. Again, you are encouraged to review the policy on guessing prior to taking any exam, to ensure that you remain apprised of any changes.

### 2.4.2.7  The Syllabus of Basic Education

Similar to the SOA Education section of the website, the CAS publishes a Syllabus of Basic Education that contains detailed information on the exam process, including schedules, fees, examination rules, the official syllabus materials, study hints, and other information. It is available on the CAS website. I would encourage all students pursuing admission to the CAS to read the syllabus thoroughly and then review it prior to each exam offering for any material changes.

### 2.4.2.8  The Grading System

For exams 3L and 5 – 9, passing candidates are informed that they passed the exam, but are not given a grade, while unsuccessful candidates receive a score of 0 – 5. In addition, unsuccessful candidates for exams 3L and 5 – 9 will also receive a more detailed summary of their exam result for educational guidance.

### 2.4.3 The Joint Board for the Enrollment of Actuaries

The Joint Board co-sponsors the enrolled actuaries (EA) examinations with SOA and ASPPA. To attain the EA designation, you must complete the following three examinations:

- *EA-1*

  This exam is two and one half hours in length, is offered each May, and consists solely of multiple-choice (MC) questions. It tests proficiency in the following two areas:

  1. The mathematics of compound interest and financial analysis;

  2. The mathematics of life contingencies and demography.

  Candidates can earn a waiver for the EA-1 examination if they have earned a degree in actuarial science from an accredited college or university, or if they have successfully completed SOA Exams FM and MLC.

- *EA-2F*

  This exam is four hours in length, is offered each November, and consists solely of MC questions. It covers actuarial assumptions, actuarial cost methods, calculation of minimum required contributions, and calculation of maximum deductible contributions.

- *EA-2L*

  This exam is two and one-half hours in length, is offered each May, and consists solely of MC questions. It covers the relevant pension laws (in particular the provisions of the Employee Retirement Income Security Act (ERISA) and related laws, regulations, and rulings) as they affect pension actuarial practice.

One unique aspect of EA examinations is that candidates have the right to request that their individual exam sheets be returned to them after the exam. The exam sheets can be requested up to 6 months after the date of the exam. More information is available from the Joint Board website.

The Retirement Benefits U. S. Fellowship track of the SOA requires that candidates complete the EA exams, in addition to the other more general requirements for Associateship and Fellowship. Thus, students interested in pursuing careers in Defined Benefits and related disciplines in the U. S. are strongly encouraged to consider earning the FSA designation.

For more information on the enrolled actuaries examinations or the EA designation, read the Examination Program, available on the Joint Board website (www.irs.gov/taxpros/actuaries/) and the SOA website (www.soa.org/).

### 2.4.4 The Canadian Institute of Actuaries

Although a separate body in a separate nation, the CIA does not administer its own independent examinations. Instead, it jointly sponsors the exam systems of the SOA and the CAS for the basic education of Canadian actuaries. Due, however, to the relatively minor portion of Canadian-specific material on the syllabi of the SOA examinations, the CIA has instituted its Practice Education Course (**PEC**) for candidates educated in the SOA system. The PEC is a three-day program designed to provide Canadian actuaries with knowledge of industry practices, professional standards, and legislation specific to Canada. The PEC is not required for candidates educated in the CAS system, assuming they completed the Canadian-specific version of CAS Exam 6.

An alternative route to the Fellow, Canadian Institute of Actuaries (**FCIA**) designation is through a Mutual Recognition Agreement (**MRA**). The CIA has MRAs with certain other global actuarial organizations, which stipulate that candidates having completed the educational requirements of those organizations can attain an FCIA designation by completing the PEC and satisfying a few additional requirements, including a course on professionalism and a specified amount of Canada-focused work experience. More details are available on the CIA website.

Effective in 2012, the CIA began its University Accreditation Program (**UAP**), which will provide university students with the potential to achieve exemptions from exams FM/2, MFE/3F, MLC/3L, and C/4 upon attainment of a minimum grade in specific courses from accredited universities. It is the belief of the CIA that this program will increase the predictability of FCIA "travel time."

### 2.4.5 The American Academy of Actuaries

Apart from the exam requirements associated with earning membership status in the SOA, CAS, or other acceptable actuarial organization (which is required for the MAAA designation), there are no formal examination requirements for joining the AAA.

## 2.5 ACTUARIAL TRAINING PROGRAMS

When hired, aspiring actuaries will most likely participate in an employer-sponsored actuarial training program. While the specifics vary from company to company, the general characteristics are as follows:

1. Candidates will receive a block of paid time, typically from 120-150 hours per exam sitting, that may be used to study during work hours. The additional time required to study is generally uncompensated;

2. There is an additional level of financial support (varying by company) for actuarial exams, which may include paid exam fees, textbooks, calculators, study manuals, seminars, and other expenses. There is usually a limit on these expenditures, and they will usually vary according to a candidate's rate of success (e.g. in some companies a candidate must pay the exam fees out-of-pocket for any exam that was previously failed);

3. There is often a rotational component to an actuarial job, which involves successive job changes every 12-24 months until fellowship is achieved. These programs are designed to ensure that you have a wide variety of experience with various actuarial job functions prior to earning Fellowship (somewhat similar to the corresponding practice in the medical field);

4. There is typically a system of structured bonuses and/or pay increases corresponding to exam and job success. The system is designed to motivate employees to achieve success on exams as well as in the workplace, and to reward them for the development of actuarial competencies.

Upon completion of the credentialing process, employees will typically "graduate" from the program and settle into a semi-permanent position in the company that corresponds to corporate needs, as well as employees' chosen specialty track and area(s) of expertise.

Participation in an actuarial training program allows aspiring actuaries to progress through the educational process with financial support while gaining professional experience. Though uniquely challenging to navigate, actuarial training programs are usually designed to optimize advancement through the beginning stages of an actuarial career both efficiently and effectively.

## 2.6   RESOURCES

Following is a list of resources for aspiring or current actuaries in the U.S. and Canada.

1.  www.beanactuary.org

    This website, jointly developed by the SOA and the CAS, contains a wealth of information regarding the actuarial profession, including a description of the field, a basic overview of the education process, sample examinations, a description of programs for minority students wishing to become actuaries, salary information, and a set of related links. It is an excellent place to begin for those interested in the career.

2.  www.soa.org

    The official website of the Society of Actuaries.

3.  www.casact.org

    The official website of the Casualty Actuarial Society.

4.  www.actuary.org

    The official website of the American Academy of Actuaries.

5. www.asppa.org

   The official website of The American Society of Pension Professionals and Actuaries.

6. www.irs.gov/taxpros/actuaries

   The official website of the Joint Board for the Enrollment of Actuaries.

7. www.actuaries.ca

   The official website of the Canadian Institute of Actuaries.

8. www.bls.gov/oco

   The official website of the U.S. Department of Labor, containing the future projected job outlook for actuaries, salary information, descriptions of actuarial work and employers, and other information.

9. www.ccactuaries.org

   The official website of the Conference of Consulting Actuaries, a professional organization devoted to serving actuaries employed in consulting firms.

10. www.blackactuaries.org

   The official website of the International Association of Black Actuaries, an organization committed to supporting Black actuarial students and professionals by instituting mentoring and career development initiatives.

11. www.imageoftheactuary.org

A site devoted to promoting actuaries to employers and the general public.

12. http://blog.soa.org

A dialog about SOA and the actuarial profession

13. www.actuarialfoundation.org

The Foundation focuses on education and research programs in the U. S. that serve the public.

# 3

# ℙRELIMINARY ACTUARIAL EXAMINATIONS

## 3.1 BACKGROUND

This chapter is intended to cover the preliminary exams, all of which contain highly mathematical content. With respect to the SOA, this chapter corresponds to Exams P, FM, MLC, MFE, and C under the current system. With respect to the CAS, this chapter corresponds to Exams 1-4 under the current system. It also covers the EA-1 exam, and loosely, EA-2A and EA-2B, which are multiple choice exams but not necessarily purely mathematical in content.

It is likely that you will find some of the strategies and guidelines discussed in this chapter to be common sense. This is expected, as the preliminary exam structure is relatively straightforward, and the repertoire of sound study methods discussed is relatively conventional. Much of the information presented may, however, prove to be new or may serve to supplement existing study fundamentals.

## 3.2 PROBLEMS, PROBLEMS, PROBLEMS

The preliminary exams afford two very important luxuries to the aspiring actuary that the fellowship exams do not. First, the topics covered by these exams are rooted in mathematical, statistical, and actuarial fundamentals that have remained mostly static for a long period of time. As a result, there is a vast history of past exam questions with which to practice that is readily available at a reasonable cost. Past exams can be downloaded from many of the official actuarial websites and are printed in any quality commercially published study manual.

Second, preliminary exams are generally administered several times annually (especially those exams offered in computer-based format), whereas the fellowship exams are usually administered only once or twice annually. These luxuries ultimately translate into the availability of a plethora of past exam questions (usually with detailed solutions), in some cases more than the student has time to use.

This abundance of problems presents several critical advantages. First, students who best learn by example will be able to do so without the worry of depleting the question bank. Second, students who repetitively solve hundreds of problems from the same topic material not only gain a general theoretical understanding of that material, but also of the *types* or *patterns* of questions that are asked for a given topic. With sufficient practice, you will be able to quickly recognize and distinguish between various types of questions on exam day. Though it is certainly true that a question-writer may develop a problem with an obscure or uncommon formulation, your chances of encountering a truly foreign problem type on an exam decline dramatically as the number of problems practiced increases. Third, "learning by doing" conforms nicely with many students' intuitive understanding of their own styles. It has been my experience as an educator that many classroom students concentrate very heavily on the lecture delivery, but do not truly grasp the conceptual underpinnings until an example is done. The analogy to actuarial exams is clear, and the enormity of past question banks makes this easy.

In general, doing as many problems as many times as possible has long been regarded as the core fundamental preparation strategy for preliminary exams, and there is no obvious reason why this should change anytime in the near future. Whenever possible, but especially in the weeks immediately prior to the exam, take practice exams under simulated (and appropriately timed) exam conditions, and grade your overall performance after each. Be sure to review the solutions to any problems you were unable to solve; this will allow you to identify and address opportunities for improvement.

I stress the importance of taking *timed* practice exams, as opposed to simply doing practice problems. Many students do problems for stretches of only an hour or two, despite the fact that preliminary exams can be as long as four hours. These students underestimate the impact that additional time can have on their ability to concentrate. "Exam stamina" will be a crucial factor in your ability to perform well on the latter portions of the exam.

## 3.3 FORMULA/SHORTCUT MEMORIZATION

Many students struggle with striking a proper balance between memorizing formulas and finding computational shortcuts, versus relying on the ability to derive important formulaic results as needed. The human brain has memory limitations (at least mine does), and sometimes, struggling to force as many formulas and shortcuts as possible into your memory can prove to be counterproductive, as well as risky, especially if the reliance is solely on memory. What if you forget an important formula on an exam? What if a problem is different in a very small way, forcing you to solve it from first principles without the use of a "canned" formula? All of these factors point toward reliance on derivation as the more appropriate choice. There is, however, a considerable time tradeoff, since deriving important formulaic results during exam conditions can be very time-consuming. What if the derivation is done incorrectly, or cannot be done at all, as is often the case under the pressure of exam conditions?

My recommendation is to memorize important formulas that cannot be derived with confidence in a very short amount of time. It is important, however, to note that reliance *solely* on memorization is imprudent. The appropriate strategy, therefore, is to allocate sufficient time for memorizing formulas while preserving considerable time for understanding their derivations. Here are a few guidelines to assist you in properly apportioning your time to achieve this goal:

1. Review the derivation given in the text and/or study manual for every formula committed to memory;

2. Replicate this derivation without the references;

3. Do not memorize special cases of a general formula even if they are presented separately, unless it is absolutely necessary to do so.

   For example, the formula $(1+i) = \dfrac{1}{1-d}$

   is just a special case of the formula $\left(1+\dfrac{i^{(m)}}{m}\right)^{m} = \left(1-\dfrac{d^{(n)}}{n}\right)^{-n}$

   where $m = n = 1$, but many study materials segregate them;

4. In the early stages of preparation, whenever possible, solve a practice problem first using a formula from memory and again using first principles. This will prepare you to solve an exam question in both ways, should an instance arise in which one of your methods fails.

In short, memorizing formulas should be done *as a supplement to*, but not *in lieu of*, developing a solid conceptual understanding of the relevant concepts.

## 3.4 COMMERCIAL STUDY MANUALS

Actuarial students have been relying on commercial study manuals for decades. Their use goes hand-in-hand with the ideas presented here, since it is in study manuals that students are likely to find large depositories of questions and detailed solutions, as well as summaries of important formulas. I would recommend that every student taking actuarial exams purchase a study manual. There are a large number of study manuals and other study products on the market; each has a unique writing style and organization of content. This can often make a prudent choice difficult.

Here are some factors to consider in choosing a study manual:

1. Fellow students may be able to provide valuable advice regarding study manuals, particularly if those students' learning styles are similar to yours;

2. It is generally easy to find old copies of study manuals, or to download samples from the manual off the internet, which can be reviewed for quality. Beware, however, that an old manual may not be indicative of the quality of a current edition if the manual's author has changed;

3. Beware of study manuals whose promises are too aggressive, particularly if those manuals are in their first edition.

## 3.5 CALCULATOR PROFICIENCY

Mastery of your calculator is an undervalued skill, the importance of which cannot be overstated. In many cases, you will be able to considerably reduce the time you spend obtaining an answer to a computational problem by developing suitable proficiency with your calculator. In general, for time conservation purposes, writing may be reduced significantly with proper use of memory keys. In addition, many calculators possess powerful functions of which some exam takers may be unaware. This is especially true with regard to the following:

1. Financial calculators can directly calculate the present value, future value, or payment of an annuity given the other variables. It is therefore not necessary to solve analytically for these quantities. In addition, financial calculators have the power to solve for the interest rate in many equations of value, eliminating the need to iteratively solve for such a variable. In recent years, permissible calculators have evolved to the point where they can solve for financial quantities of interest even in cases in which the payment stream is non-level or erratic in either the amount or timing of payments. The TI BA II Plus$^{©}$ is an excellent calculator, particularly for financially oriented questions. In addition, there are several other permissible calculators with comparable functionality, a list of which can be obtained on the SOA or CAS website.

2. Statistical analysis functions of most scientific calculators are capable of calculating many distribution descriptors, such as the mean, median, and standard deviation of a sample. Many are also capable of solving for regression coefficients and other quantities of interest in applied statistics.

As technology progresses, it is likely that the calculators permitted for use in actuarial exams will become more powerful and will be capable of more sophisticated calculations. Learning to maximize the effectiveness of your calculator is an imperative step in the study process that will pay countless dividends under exam conditions. After all, acquiring the knowledge and expertise necessary to answer every question on the exam would be a worthless exercise if you could only complete 40% of the problems in the allotted time!

This is so critical that the syllabus for the Financial Mathematics exam offered by the SOA includes Study Notes on the effective use of the TI BA II Plus. Thus calculator proficiency will be assumed in the construction of this exam.

Be advised that you are generally permitted to bring multiple calculators to exams. For this reason, you are encouraged to bring the TI BA II Plus as well as a scientific calculator that is approved for exam use.

## 3.6   BACK-SOLVING

Preliminary examinations afford another very valuable luxury to the actuarial student that fellowship exams do not. This is the prospect of **back-solving** an exam question when you lack the ability to solve the problem directly.

To illustrate one application of back-solving, consider the following example. In the beginning stages of my career (back when calculus was still tested in the credentialing process), I routinely relied upon back-solving to correctly answer questions pertaining to differential equations. Rather than solve the differential equation for the appropriate function, I would take the derivatives of the functions given as answer choices and plug them in to the equation, choosing the one that satisfied it.

For example, suppose the differential equation to be solved is

$$\frac{d^2y}{dx^2} - 3\frac{dy}{dx} + 2y = 0,$$

and the answer choices are given as

(A)   $y = e^{2x}$

(B)   $y = e^{3x}$

(C)   $y = e^{4x}$

(D)   $y = e^{5x}$

(E)   $y = e^{6x}$

Rather than directly solving this problem, suppose you guessed answer choice (A). Noting that

$$\frac{dy}{dx} = 2e^{2x} \text{ and } \frac{d^2y}{dx^2} = 4e^{2x},$$

you can verify that

$$\frac{d^2y}{dx^2} - 3\frac{dy}{dx} + 2y = 4e^{2x} - 3(2e^{2x}) + 2e^{2x} = 0,$$

and therefore, that you have guessed correctly.

Another application of back-solving is when you are able to understand the question and formulate the expression required to answer it, but you are unable to solve for the variable of interest. Suppose a question reads, "At what effective rate of interest would the present value of 1 paid at time 4, and 6 paid at time 8 be equal to 2?" In working the problem, you correctly write the equation of value as

$$6v^8 + v^4 = 2.$$

The proper way to isolate the variable $i$ is to rewrite the equation as

$$6(v^4)^2 + v^4 - 2 = 0,$$

and use the quadratic formula to solve for $v^4 = .50$. Then, the effective rate can be obtained from

$$i = \frac{1}{\left(v^4\right)^{1/4}} - 1 = \frac{1}{.50^{1/4}} - 1 = 18.92\%.$$

If you did not recognize this as a quadratic equation, however, you could still solve this problem by back-solving. Suppose the answer choices were:

(A)  18.72%

(B)  18.92%

(C)  19.12%

(D)  19.32%

(E)  19.52%.

You could then substitute each of these possible answer choices into the equation of value to determine which satisfies it. In situations such as this, it is preferable to start with choice (C), since the result will indicate in which direction you ought to guess next if (C) is not correct. In this example, if you had guessed choice (C) first, you would have obtained a value less than 2 for the left-hand-side of the equation; this would cause you to subsequently guess a lower interest rate in order to increase your present value to 2. You have a 20% chance of getting the correct answer on the first guess, but even if you guess incorrectly, you have a 100% chance of determining the correct answer based upon the results of your next guess. Remember, you have eliminated choices (D) and (E) based on the results of your first guess. Therefore, the answer is either (A) or (B), and regardless of which you actually guess next, you will know after your check which is correct. Even if determining the correct answer takes two guesses, it is sometimes more efficient than solving an exam question directly!

I again caution you to make a judicious first guess, since a poorly chosen initial guess may make identifying the correct answer a very time consuming process. If, for example, your initial guess was (E), the left-hand side of the equation would be less than 2, indicating that a lower interest rate needs to be selected. This finding presents you with no additional information regarding which of (A), (B), (C), or (D) might represent an appropriate change in rate.

Effectively implementing this strategy, of course, is only possible if guessing allows you to determine the exact answer choice. This will usually be the case if the answer choices are numbers (such as in the example above), and will generally also be the case if the answer choices are non-overlapping intervals, such as the following:

(A)   Less than 18.80%
(B)   Greater than 18.80%, but less than 19.20%
(C)   Greater than 19.20%, but less than 19.40%
(D)   Greater than 19.40%, but less than 19.60%
(E)   Greater than 19.60%.

There is, of course, a significant time risk associated with back-solving if the equation into which you are substituting the answers is complicated, or if the time required to check even one answer choice is prohibitively long (e.g. a fifth-order differential equation). As always, whether or not the time required to back-solve is worth spending depends on the characteristics of the specific problem in question, the situation in which it is encountered, and the total time you have available to spend on any particular question.

## 3.7 SYLLABUS MATERIAL VS. SUPPLEMENTS

The published syllabus material is the foundation for all actuarial exams, and familiarity with it is an absolute *requirement* for success. I have found anecdotally, though, that successful preliminary exam candidates generally devote a smaller *proportion* of their preparation time to direct study from the official syllabus references, and a larger proportion to other activities, such as doing practice problems, taking practice exams, memorizing formulas, and doing other miscellaneous exam-preparation activities. In many cases the ratio can be as much as 2 or 3 to 1, highlighting the importance of extensive practice to passing exams. An exception to this theme is when the syllabus references themselves contain valuable end-of-chapter exercises or other quality review items, in which case the ratio may not be quite as high.

## 3.8 ON EXAM DAY

### ▶ Time Management

Prior to beginning each exam, calculate the number of minutes allocated to each question. A 4-hour exam containing 40 questions is implicitly allocating 6 minutes per question. During the exam, periodically check to ensure that you are properly pacing yourself. In this scenario, after 1 hour has passed, you should have completed at least 10 questions.

Make a first pass through the exam, solving the straightforward questions first. If you have spent the allotted time on one question, and are not very close to the answer, move on to the next question. Resist the temptation to solve a problem at all costs; it will harm you in the longer run even if you ultimately succeed in obtaining the solution to that specific problem. You can always revisit unsolved questions later as time permits.

If you have prepared properly, you should be able to solve many of the questions on your first pass in far less than the allotted time. Then, continue to make subsequent passes though the exam, progressively solving harder problems. Use the time saved on your first pass to help you answer the more involved questions on subsequent passes.

### ▶ Bring More than One Calculator and Pencil

Having backup pencils and calculators may seem like a baseline expectation to many students, but surprisingly, I have witnessed dozens of students enter the examination room unequipped with such devices. Do not jeopardize your chances of success on an exam for which you have studied for several hundred hours, and on which future salary increases and professional respect depend, by failing to properly procure basic "school supplies!" Bring at least five pencils and two calculators. If you are taking an exam on paper, make sure the lead in your pencils corresponds to the allowable darkness indicated (most of the time, #2 pencils suffice). You should also bring a separate, clean eraser in case you have to change your answer on the Scantron sheet (stray or incompletely erased marks may create problems in grading your exam).

Make sure that at least one of your calculators is battery-powered, as opposed to solar-powered, to reduce the risk that insufficient lighting conditions will impact its functionality. This is particularly true if you are taking the exam at an examination center with which you are unfamiliar.

## ►Computer-Based Testing (CBT)

Computer-based testing was introduced to the SOA and CAS actuarial exam process in September 2005 for Exam P/1, and has since been expanded to several more preliminary exams. Exams P, FM, MFE and C are now only available through CBT in most locations, while SOA exam MLC, CAS exams 3L, 3LC, 3ST, 5, and 6, and the EA exams continue to be offered in a paper-based format. In addition to the benefit of more frequent administrations of CBT exams, you will receive an unofficial pass/fail result immediately upon completion of the exam.

If you have never taken a computer-based test in a testing center, you should definitely practice prior to sitting for your actuarial exam. It is very important that you be completely familiar with the process before you sit for the actual exam. You can take a 30 minute test drive, in which you can experience a complete run through of the testing process, including the scheduling, registration, and check-in processes, introduction to test center staff and surroundings, and a live 15-minute generic sample test demonstrating the testing process itself. The Test Drive is only available on Tuesdays from 4:00 p.m. to 5:00 p.m. local time at select test centers. There is a fee for this, but if you've never taken a test electronically, it is well worth it.

▶ **Circle Your Answer in the Exam Booklet**

While most preliminary exams are now computerized, you may still encounter some that are offered on paper. In this case, I strongly encourage you to circle your answer choices in the exam booklet in addition to marking them on the Scantron sheet. You should also do any written work in the exam booklet on the relevant question's page. In the unlikely event that your answer sheet is lost, graders may refer to your exam booklet to determine the answers that likely appeared on your Scantron sheet. It will also help you in the event that you are forced to reconcile your answers with your Scantron sheet, as I describe in the next section.

▶ **Monitor the Recording of Your Answers**

Preliminary exams that are offered on paper are still electronically graded. I once fell victim to every actuarial student's worst nightmare - I completed a 40-question examination, and was ready to darken the letter next to #40 on my Scantron answer sheet, only to discover that #40 had already been filled in (presumably with my answer to #39). Nausea immediately ensued. I quickly scanned (no pun intended) my answer sheet for blanks, hoping to find my error quickly. I immediately saw that I had skipped the set of bubbles corresponding to #33. Checking my answers from the actual examination workbook against the darkened letters from #1 to #32 confirmed that my error had been made when I darkened a circle in #34 that was supposed to have been darkened in #33. Since seven of my answers now corresponded with the wrong questions, I thoroughly erased and re-darkened those that needed correction (I saved a little time at one point by virtue of the fact that I was answering "D" for four consecutive questions).

Luckily, my error had been made late in the exam, and I had made timely progress throughout the period. As a result, I had sufficient time to repair this almost-tragedy. But let this incident serve as a warning to you – always double-check your answer sheet or the answers you entered with CBT to ensure that the response that you give corresponds to the question you are intending to answer! Taking a split-second to perform this all-important check is an absolute must. Trust me; it is good for your stomach as well as your career.

## ►Guessing

There is currently no penalty for guessing on *most* preliminary actuarial exams. This means that you can maximize your performance by answering every question. Make sure, however, that you are aware of the official policy on guessing for any exam that you are going to take.

The particular methodology used by actuarial students to guess tends to vary greatly. On questions for which you are able to exclude one or more of the answer choices, choosing the one most closely aligned with your intuition is obviously preferred. For absolute guessing, when you are unable to make any progress toward the correct answer choice, there are different schools of thought. Absolute guessing usually takes place near the end of the exam, after the proctor announces that the examination is almost over. Students scramble to fill in guesses to the questions on which they made no progress. My approach was to determine the particular letter that had served as my answer to the fewest already-completed questions, and to use that letter for all of my guesses. If, for example, I had answered 30 questions, and I had used letters "A," "B," "C," and "D" seven times each and letter "E" only twice, I would choose letter "E" for all of the remaining questions.

There are many equally unscientific methods used by students to assign guesses to questions on actuarial exams. Many students, for example, use one letter to serve for the response to all of the questions on which they randomly guess ("C" is the most common). If you believe that the probability of any given letter serving as the correct answer is 0.2, and that individual questions are independent, then any benefits from the particular methodology chosen for guessing are not, and can not, be apparent in advance. If you have a "hunch" about guessing, there does not seem to be any scientific reason to discourage your use of it.

Whatever you decide, you must comprehend the unfortunate reality that the accuracy of your guesses can often make the difference between passing and failing an examination, particularly if you are a borderline candidate on a preliminary exam. This can be a particularly unnerving reality, especially since the accuracy of your guesses is out of your control. It can be extremely disconcerting to contemplate the possibility that a marginally well-prepared candidate might pass, and a better-prepared candidate (such as you) might fail, solely due to the chance factor introduced by guessing.

One way to cope with these feelings is to regard this matter as "out of your hands." There will always be the occasional fluke; for example, I once knew a student who analytically solved 5 questions on a 20-question exam, and guessed on the remaining 15 questions, only to get a 6! But by and large, students should not expect the quality of their guesses to be any different from that of their peers. The best way to cope with these feelings is to prepare so thoroughly for an exam (using the techniques in this book, of course), that the number of questions for which you are required to guess is equal (or close) to zero.

Some exams have penalized candidates for guessing by awarding 1/5 of a point for every answer choice left blank. In this case, whether or not you should guess depends upon two factors:

1.  The number of answer choices you can eliminate with confidence;

2.  Your performance on the rest of the exam.

If you feel strongly about your performance on the rest of the exam, you will likely find it less effective to guess randomly on questions for which you are unable to confidently exclude any answer choices, since the extra fractional points from blank answer choices will provide a cushion for your success. If you do not feel overly confident about your performance on the rest of the exam, you might find it crucial to guess randomly, since by failing to guess you will seal your fate. After all, even the longest odds of success by guessing are preferred to surefire failure.

You are reminded to be sure to double-check the policy on guessing prior to taking each exam.

## 3.9 EA EXAMS

While the basic advice that applies to preliminary examinations applies equally to the EA examinations, there are also some additional items pertaining to the structure of the questions on those exams that deserve mention here.

### ►General

As the EA examinations continue to be administered on paper, I recommend (consistent with the advice earlier in this chapter) that you record the answers (as well as the accompanying work) to all multiple choice questions in the test booklet as well as on the "bubble" sheet. This is particularly important in the event that you must later reconcile your answers due to entering an answer on the wrong line. It will also come in handy in the unlikely event that your Scantron sheet is lost and graders must rely on your test booklet to score your exam.

There are often questions that test seemingly peripheral topics or which contain words or concepts with which you are unfamiliar. If this happens, don't panic. Just do your best and move on. These questions cover such a wide cross-section of the material, some of it obscure, that it is very difficult to do them all correctly. Focus your preparation time on recognizing and being familiar with the types of questions you will likely encounter, each of which is covered in the following section.

### ►Computational

These are simply mathematical exercises that require you to carry out a short sequence of calculations to obtain a numeric answer. These are generally straightforward questions and not much more can be said, other than to ensure that you do not spend too much time on any one question.

### ►Multiple Matching

Multiple matching questions provide you with two items, labeled X and Y, and three properties, labeled I, II, and III. You must then determine which of the properties correspond to which of the items. In each question, either X or Y is related to exactly two of the properties.

The answer key for these questions generally resembles the following:

| Lettered Item | | Is Related to Numbered Items |
|---|---|---|
| (A) | X | I and II only |
| (B) | X | II and III only |
| (C) | Y | I and II only |
| (D) | Y | I and III only |

(E)  The correct answer is not given by (A), (B), (C), or (D).

Note, however, that the key is not always equal to that shown above, and the answer choices do not necessarily appear in the order above. Therefore, it is important to review the key for each individual question prior to marking your answer sheet rather than relying upon the prototype above.

To illustrate, consider an actual question from a past exam.

X.  Captive Agents

Y.  Banks

I.  Commission overrides

II.  Streamlined underwriting and issue processes

III. Life insurance for estate planning

Since captive agents are related to commission overrides and life insurance for estate planning, and banks are related to streamlined underwriting and issue processes, you determine that X is related to I and III only. This corresponds to letter choice (E), since none of the other choices encompass this relationship.

Here are some general guidelines to help you most effectively handle multiple matching questions:

1.  Draw lines from X and Y to the properties as you reason them out, since it is surprisingly easy to forget what conclusions you reached on previous items as you think about the later ones;

2.  Assuming the answer choice legend given above, notice that either of the following situations will trigger answer choice (E):

    i.   X is related to I and III
    ii.  Y is related to II and III

Therefore, if you must guess randomly on a given multiple matching question, this fact may influence your guess if you believe that all combinations of relationships are equally likely.

### ►Assertion / Reason

Assertion / Reason questions provide you with two statements. One is labeled "Assertion," and the other is labeled "Reason." First, you will be required to determine if both of these statements are true or false. Additionally, if both statements are determined to be true, you must also determine if the statement labeled "Reason" is a correct explanation of the statement labeled "Assertion," or if they are independently true.

The answer key for these questions generally resembles the following:

(A)  Both the assertion and reason are true statements, and the reason is a correct explanation of the assertion

(B)  Both the assertion and reason are true statements, but the reason is NOT a correct explanation of the assertion

(C)  The assertion is a true statement, but the reason is a false statement

(D)  The assertion is a false statement, but the reason is a true statement

(E)  Both the assertion and reason are false statements.

Again, however, you are reminded to review the key for each individual question prior to marking your answer sheet rather than relying upon the prototype above.

As an example, consider this question from an SOA Examination:

| Assertion | | Reason |
|---|---|---|
| Proponents of the efficient market hypothesis do not advocate technical analysis. | **Because** | Technical analysis relies on earnings and dividend prospects, expectation of future interest rates, and and risk evaluation. |

Since the assertion is a true statement and the reason is a false statement, the student determined that the correct response was (C).

In doing assertion/reason questions, it is my recommendation that you write a "T" or "F" next to each statement in the exam booklet as you determine its truthfulness, since it is very easy to forget your prior conclusions while concentrating on the remaining statement.

## ►True/False

These questions are identical to the typical true / false questions you have undoubtedly experienced at many times in your life. I urge you not to waste time on them. If you don't know the answer, take a few seconds to reason it out, and do your best, keeping in mind the policy for guessing.

## ►Other

The above sections describe the most commonly encountered styles of multiple choice questions asked on actuarial examinations. It is certainly possible that new question styles may emerge to further test students (and provoke additional test day anxiety). If this occurs, don't panic. Just do the best you can and move on.

## 3.10 CONCLUSION

In general, the procedures, guidelines, and tips presented in this chapter will help you significantly in preparing for the preliminary actuarial exams. You may, however, have individual personality traits, study methods, and/or learning styles that lend themselves naturally to the application of additional techniques or the substitution of other methods for those given here. While I would not recommend dramatic deviations from these procedures, it is certainly advisable for you to adapt the methodologies that best fit your learning style.

# 4
# WRITTEN ANSWER EXAMINATIONS

## 4.1 BACKGROUND

This chapter is intended to cover those exams consisting principally or entirely of written-answer (WA) questions. With respect to the SOA, this corresponds to the fellowship exams. With respect to the CAS, it applies to Exams 5-9. "Written-answer" refers not only to essay-style questions in which no computational work is required, but also to questions for which an appropriate answer contains some longhand computations or application of formulas.

In this chapter, I address each type of written-answer question and explain the optimal way to formulate your answer to each. In addition, I also discuss general themes associated with preparation for Fellowship exams and give a few tips from some experienced actuarial students.

The SOA has released a document titled "Guide to SOA Written-Answer Exams," which is available on the SOA website and contains suggestions for improving performance. I would recommend you review that document in addition to the information put forth here.

## 4.2  COMPUTATIONAL PROBLEMS

### 4.2.1  Introduction to Computational Problems

There is a significant difference between the approach that ought to be used to formulate an answer to a computational problem for a preliminary exam, and the approach that ought to be used for a written answer question. In a preliminary exam for which all questions are multiple-choice, the only important element of your solution is the final answer. Regardless of your level of preparation or expertise in a given topic, the only proof of your educational progress weighed by the computer (or graders in the case of paper-based exams) is the proportion of questions answered correctly. This is an all-or-nothing approach, which only rewards answers that are 100% correct and implicitly disallows partial credit. Sloppiness in writing numbers or symbols, incorrect notation, skipping intermediate steps, and failing to deduce your answer in a logical order, while less than ideal in an objective sense, are unimportant so long as they do not impede your ability to obtain the correct end result.

For the more advanced exams, this situation is completely reversed. Exam papers are individually graded by volunteer actuaries. Graders employ grading outlines to assign points to a given candidate for a given question. The grading outline lists each step in the solution to the problem and assigns it a point value. The point value is not important in an absolute sense, it is only important in a relative sense. A step in the question that is worth three points, for example, should be three times as important in the solution as a step worth only 1 point. Steps generally considered more important than others include those indicating knowledge of major themes or formulas essential for successfully calculating the quantities required or performing the analysis requested. Steps generally considered to be of negligible importance are the actual numerical computations and peripheral details/enhancements of the solution. Arithmetic errors, for example, tend not to be penalized heavily. Note also that the "points" on the grading outline have no relationship to the official "point value" of a given question on the exam. A 3-point question on the exam might have 50 total points on the grading outline, while an 8-point question on the exam might only have 40 total points on the grading outline.

The possible points on the outline for any given question are relative only to that question and are not used for cross-question comparisons.

## 4.2.2 Writing Relevant Formulas/Procedures

Suppose the following multi-part, computational problem appeared on a fellowship exam:

> Jones flips a biased coin 10 times. The probability of observing a head on the biased coin is .55. If all flips are independent:
>
> (a) Compute the probability that Jones will flip exactly 6 heads;
>
> (b) Compute the probability that Jones will flip at least 1 head.

Note that it is extremely unlikely that a question of an elementary nature such as this would appear on a higher-level exam. It was chosen as an example merely because its topic is understood by the vast majority of actuarial exam takers, and is therefore useful for demonstrative purposes.

The grading outline for this question might be as shown in Figure 4.1. Note the setup of this grading outline. It awards the most points for knowledge of the binomial distribution and of an elementary rule of probability. The next most important concept is the ability to select the correct data to apply in the calculations. Very few points are awarded for actually performing the numerical calculations. This probably makes good intuitive sense; if you are very familiar with the binomial distribution and its parameters, you should not be penalized heavily, for example, if you accidentally make a silly mistake on your calculator. After all, the goal of the examiner is to test your knowledge of the binomial distribution and understanding of complementary events; the exact mechanics of the appropriate computations, while important, pale in comparison to general knowledge of the subject.

| Step | Points |
|---|---|
| For the binomial distribution, the probability of getting $k$ "successes" in $n$ independent trials if the probability of success on any one trial is $p$ is $$f(k) = {}_nC_k(p)^k(1-p)^{n-k},$$ where $${}_nC_k = \frac{n!}{k!(n-k)!}$$ | 5 |
| Here, $$n = 10, p = .55$$ | 2 |
| For part (a), $$f(6) = {}_{10}C_6(.55)^6(1-.55)^4 = .2384$$ | 1 |
| **Part (a) subtotal** | **8** |
| For part (b), we first note that for any event $E$, $$P(E) = 1 - P(E^C)$$ | 3 |
| Therefore, $P$(at least one head) $= 1 - P$(less than one head) $= 1 - P$(zero heads) $= 1 - {}_{10}C_0(p)^0(1-p)^{10}$ | 2 |
| So, $$P(\text{zero heads}) = (.45)^{10} = .000341$$ | 1 |
| So $$P(\text{at least one head}) = 1 - .000341 = .999659$$ | 1 |
| **Part (b) subtotal** | **7** |
| **TOTAL POINTS** | **15** |

**FIGURE 4.1**

Obviously, if your answer were identical to the grading outline above, you would be awarded all 15 points for this question. You need not, however, give the "model" answer above in order to obtain full credit for the question. The solution shown in Figure 4.2 would also likely yield 15 points:

| Step | Points |
|---|---|
| For part (a), $f(6) = {}_{10}C_6(.55)^6(1-.55)^4 = .2384$ | 8 |
| $P$(at least one head) $= 1-(1-.55)^{10} = .99659$ | 7 |
| **TOTAL POINTS** | 15 |

**FIGURE 4.2**

Despite the fact that this answer does not contain the full density function for the binomial distribution, an identification of variables, or an explanation of the rules of probability required, it will be awarded full credit since it indicates an understanding of all facets of the question. Writing an answer in this format, however, is extremely dangerous, as will be illustrated in the following hypothetical example.

Consider two equally prepared students, Unwise and Wise, both of whom know how to do the question correctly. Each student makes a silly error in part (b) by accidentally using .45 for $p$ rather than .55, since they are thinking in terms of complements and just mix up the numbers (such a mistake is very easy to make under exam conditions, particularly for a student who is pressed for time).

Suppose that Unwise's answer for part (b) is as shown in Figure 4.3.

| Step | Points |
|---|---|
| So $P$(at least one head) $= 1-(1-.45)^{10} = .997467$ | 0 |
| **TOTAL POINTS FOR PART (b)** | 0 |

**FIGURE 4.3**

In other words, she failed to disclose the formulas or describe the procedures she was utilizing to solve the problem. This places the grader in a very difficult situation; he would like to believe that Unwise knew the correct formulas and that her error was merely an absent-minded mistake, but how can he be sure? There is no indication that appropriate formulas were used, nor is there any indication that

Unwise knew the proper treatment of complementary events (and it is not common for graders to award points on the basis of speculation!). It is therefore impossible for the grader to determine whether Unwise lacked knowledge of the problem or if she merely made an input mistake. The grader has no choice but to award zero points to Unwise.

By contrast, suppose that Wise fully documents her answer, as shown in Figure 4.4.

| Step | Points |
|:---:|:---:|
| For part (b), we first note that for any event $E$, $$P(E) = 1 - P(E^C)$$ | 3 |
| $P$(at least one head) $$= 1 - P \text{ (less than one head)}$$ $$= {}_{10}C_0(p)^0(1-p)^{10}$$ | 2 |
| So, $P$(zero heads) $= (.55)^{10} = .002533$ | 0 |
| So, $P$(at least one head) $= 1 - .002533 = .997467$ | 1 |
| **TOTAL POINTS FOR PART (b)** | **6** |

**FIGURE 4.4**

Notice that Wise lost only one point, since her mistake was made solely in the calculation of $P$ (zero heads). It is clear to the grader that she possessed the requisite knowledge for successfully answering the question, and that her only mistake was an input error corresponding to the value of $p$. Note also that she still receives a point for the last line of the solution, since this calculation is correct *given the incorrect calculation in the preceding line*. Wise has received 6 points (as opposed to Unwise's 0 points), despite their having made the identical error, solely due to the manner in which their solutions were presented.

This example demonstrates how easy it can be for two candidates to achieve a considerably different score for a question despite the similarity of their knowledge bases/solutions. A carefully explained answer with appropriate formulaic disclosure that progresses in a logical fashion maximizes your potential score, while incomplete answers make you susceptible to underachievement.

### 4.2.3 Salvaging a Question

Now suppose Unwise and Wise face a different situation – neither of them can recall the density function for the binomial distribution.

Unwise decides that since the binomial density function is a necessity for both parts of this problem, attempting to answer it is futile. Her answer is shown in Figure 4.5.

| Step | Points |
|---|---|
| For part (a), ? | 0 |
| For part (b), ? | 0 |
| **TOTAL POINTS** | **0** |

**FIGURE 4.5**

Wise, however, recognizes that her lack of knowledge of the binomial distribution does not preclude her earning points for other elements of the solution. Her answer is shown in Figure 4.6.

| Step | Points |
|---|---|
| For part (a), $n = 10$, $p = .55$ | 1 |
| For part (b), we first note that for any event $E$, $P(E) = 1 - P(E^C)$ | 3 |
| Since I don't know how to calculate it, just suppose that $P(\text{zero heads}) = .30$ | 0 |
| So $P(\text{at least one head}) = 1 - .30 = .70$ | 1 |
| **TOTAL POINTS** | **5** |

**FIGURE 4.6**

Wise has garnered 5 points for her ability to identify inputs to the density function and for her knowledge of the treatment of complementary events in probability. Notice that she just admitted that calculating $P$ (zero heads) was something she was incapable of doing and used an imaginary value to complete her solution.

While 5 points out of a possible 15 points is far short of stellar, it is vastly superior to the 0 points garnered by Unwise. This point differential is even more telling when viewed in light of the fact that these two students' recollections of the topics required to solve this problem were identical!

This example reemphasizes the idea that obtaining the correct "final" numerical answer is not as important as it may seem. Concentrating on those elements of a question that you know, and seeking to maximize credit for those elements, can make a significant difference in your performance. In short, make sure you get credit for what you know!

## 4.2.4 Responding to Time Pressure

Now suppose that Wise and Unwise both know how to do the problem but are running short on time. They are attempting to earn as many points as possible for the question, with the knowledge that they do not have adequate time remaining to complete it.

Unwise works as quickly as possible, frantically punching buttons on her calculator, and runs short of time just after her response to part (a) is complete. Her answer is shown in Figure 4.7.

| Step | Points |
|------|--------|
| For the binomial distribution, the probability of getting $k$ "successes" in $n$ independent trials if the probability of success on any one trial is $p$ is $$f(k) = {}_nC_k(p)^k(1-p)^{n-k},$$ where $\ {}_nC_k = \dfrac{n!}{k!(n-k)!}$ | 5 |
| Here, $\ n = 10, \ p = .55$ | 2 |
| For part (a), $$f(6) = {}_{10}C_6(.55)^6(1-.55)^4 = .2384$$ For part (b), we first note that for | 1 |
| **TOTAL POINTS** | **8** |

**FIGURE 4.7**

Wise, on the other hand, chose to focus on the portions of the problem that she viewed to be the most important. Her answer is shown in Figure 4.8.

| Step | Points |
|---|---|
| For the binomial distribution, the probability of getting $k$ "successes" in $n$ independent trials if the probability of success on any one trial is $p$ is $$f(k) = {}_nC_k(p)^k(1-p)^{n-k},$$ where $${}_nC_k = \frac{n!}{k!(n-k)!}$$ | 5 |
| Here, $n = 10,\ p = .55$ | 2 |
| For part (b), we first note that for any event $$E,\ P(E) = 1 - P(E^C)$$ | 3 |
| **TOTAL POINTS** | **10** |

**FIGURE 4.8**

Here, Wise chose not to spend time performing the actual mechanics of the calculations required for part (a), which her formulas and input identification already indicate she knows how to do. Instead, she opted to use the time to demonstrate that she knows how to probabilistically treat complementary events, assuming that in the grader's eyes, this would be a more important element of the solution. She has managed to outscore Unwise 10 to 8, despite the fact that they both knew how to do the question and spent the same amount of time doing it! Obviously, this requires some judgment regarding what elements of a solution are more important than others, but in many cases, this is obvious.

This example illustrates a general theme: you should always use exam time in the way that rightfully earns you credit for what you know, and therefore, maximizes your potential score.

## 4.3    ESSAY QUESTIONS

### 4.3.1   Introduction to Essay Questions

I use the term "essay question" to refer to a question in which an extended written answer is required. A question of this type may appear on its own, or in conjunction with a computational problem. The following three sub-sections represent a general categorization of the types of essay questions that you may encounter on an exam. The divisions are by no means scientific and do not claim to precisely represent every question on every actuarial exam. Furthermore, any question may be a combination of two or more of these types. Nonetheless, examining the questions in these three separate "buckets" is instructive.

### 4.3.2   Regurgitation Questions and the "List" Concept

The first general type of essay question appearing on upper-level actuarial exams is what I will refer to as a regurgitation or "list" question. This type of question is generally very straightforward, tests material from a specific section of the syllabus readings, and is usually the easiest type of essay question. You will generally have success on this type of question only if you are able to recognize the origin of the question within the syllabus material and recall specifics from that particular reading. Regurgitation questions representing a large chunk of material may form the basis for an entire exam question, while regurgitation questions representing smaller bodies of material may be "tacked on" to the end of a related exam question.

Consider an actual question from a prior SOA examination: "Describe the risks associated with investing in fixed income securities." On the surface, it appears to be a fairly generic question, requiring a basic understanding of fixed income investing and the related exposures. It might seem that to best answer this question, you would reflect upon the various syllabus references, recall the risks discussed in those references to the extent possible, and attempt to elaborate on each with a reasonable level of depth and precision. This approach entails some inherent risk. Considering the thousands of pages of reading in the syllabus references, it is unlikely that you would be able to remember all of the risks relevant to fixed-income investing that are mentioned.

Consider instead an alternative approach to answering regurgitation questions taken by many successful exam candidates. In preparing for the exam, one of the references candidates were supposed to read was Chapter 2 of *The Handbook of Fixed Income Securities*. The title of this chapter is "Risks Associated with Investing in Fixed Income Securities." The chapter presents the reader with a comprehensive summary of those risks, as well as a brief description of each.

Though it is impossible to be sure, it is likely that the question writer formulated the grading outline for this question from this chapter, using the risks listed there as the foundation for the answer. Though you might be able to describe such risks if they were given to you, it is generally difficult to recall each of the risks under the time constraints and pressure of exam conditions without specifically preparing for the possibility of doing so. Therefore, the idea of the "list" has been popularized.

Essentially, when you came across this section while studying for the exam, you would create a "list page." On the top, you would write "Risks Associated with Investing in Fixed Income Securities," and underline it. Below this title, you would list the risks named in the section (e.g. call risk, reinvestment risk, etc.). You could also create a flashcard from this list, with the title on the front of the card, and the list itself on the back. You would then memorize these risks in the course of your studying, going over the list repeatedly until the information was firmly mentally ingrained. You would do this for each of the sections in the syllabus readings that contained "listlike" material. You may also wish to combine related lists into one for organizational ease, in case the exam question makes it difficult to discern the reference from which it was derived. By exam time, you should have a comprehensive collection of all such lists in memory. This process would be very useful for answering the question that I cited earlier.

During the exam, when faced with a question such as the above, I would recommend taking the following approach:

1. From memory, immediately jot down all of the main points, or major headings, from the list, leaving adequate space between each for subsequent additional detail. This simple step takes very little time and can often earn you 1/3 to 2/3 of the points for a given question;

2. Return to each major heading and fill in the main supporting details, or sub-headings, from your general recollection and understanding of the material;

3. As time permits, return to each sub-heading and fill in any miscellaneous details that apply.

The hope is that the resulting answer will substantially replicate the information on the grading outline, maximizing your potential points for the question.

As this strategy has become more popular, most commercial study manuals contain a set of lists for you to use. I would, however, encourage you to check the author's collection of lists against the readings as you go, and add any new lists (or modify existing ones) to the extent necessary.

You will find that many study manuals contain dozens or even hundreds of pages of lists, and allotting ample time for memorization is truly a daunting task. If you are pressed for time, and must eliminate certain lists from the set you will memorize, be aware of the potential consequences. Some considerations are:

1. You may wish to eliminate lists pertaining to material that has been heavily tested on recent exams (although occasionally exam questions are repeated from one year to the next, presumably to foil students who use this strategy);

2. You may wish to eliminate lists pertaining to material that you understand very well, since it is likely that you will be able to provide a good answer to a question on such material even without a memorized list;

3. You may wish to eliminate all of the lists from a particularly large or bulky reference to save valuable memorization time, and hope that this section is not tested. This strategy is very risky but has the potential to pay large dividends. You should probably avoid this strategy for references that have not been tested on the exam for a considerable period of time;

4. You should probably not eliminate lists from references with seemingly obscure material, or material that is presented in bulleted format, since in many cases having a list memorized is the student's only chance of success on a question related to that reference.

The following tactics, which may be used in isolation or in conjunction, may aid in memorization:

1. You can create a flashcard for each list that must be memorized. The front of the card displays the list title, while the back contains the actual list. Though a matter of personal taste, many students find the repeated "drilling" of lists using flashcards to be a very effective memory-enhancing technique. Flashcards are sometimes available from commercial vendors, and are usually consistent in content with the list section of the corresponding study manual;

2. You may find mnemonics to be a very powerful tool in list memorization. Simply formulate a word or expression using the first letter of each item in the list. Suppose, for example, that the list were:

---
Main Issuers of High-Yield Debt
1. Original issuers
2. Fallen angels
3. Restructurings and leveraged buyouts

You could develop the mnemonic "FOR," each letter of which represents one item from the list. In some cases, creating a helpful mnemonic can be time-consuming, and it is sometimes more difficult to remember the mnemonic than the list itself! In attempting to memorize large lists with many items, however, mnemonics can be very helpful. They also have the additional advantage that by recalling the mnemonic, you are also recalling the exact number of items in the list. The most effective mnemonics are those that form a word that is related to the list, thereby making them easier to remember. Many students have even found that making comical and/or obscene mnemonics was the best way to remember them (I abstain from judgment!).

Occasionally, commercial study manuals and flashcard sets contain mnemonics for selected lists, though this is not always the case. Students already having passed a given exam may be willing to share their mnemonics. Just keep in mind, prior to using a set of mnemonics that someone else created, that mnemonics are likely to be helpful only if they are meaningful to *you*.

I wish there were a powerful secret that I could reveal which would make the memorization process quicker, easier, or less punishing. While a few lucky individuals may naturally have superior memorization capacity, for most candidates, a long, strenuous, brute force approach is likely to be the only one that bears good results. This was the case for me.

I firmly advocate the idea of committing a set of "lists" to memory, but with the understanding that this memorization is only a supplement to an existing knowledge base. In the absence of conceptual clarity with regard to the syllabus material, the time necessary to perform rote memorization of a massive set of "lists" would be better spent acquainting yourself with important concepts and computational review.

### 4.3.3 Request for Explanation

On a regurgitation question, it may be possible for you to earn some portion of the points without truly understanding the syllabus material. Simply write the main elements of the list, and even without supporting details, you may manage to garner a decent number of points.

Requests for explanation eliminate this possibility by requiring you to define and/or describe certain items, and may also request that you use your understanding of the item to evaluate a certain situation. Consider for example parts (d) and (e) of a question from an actual examination:

    (d)    Compare the payment profile of the following types of accrual bonds:

        (i)    Z-bonds
        (ii)   Z-PAC
        (iii)  Tricky Z
        (iv)  Jump-Z with cumulative sticky trigger

    (e)    Rank the accrual bonds presented in (d) according to their suitability to help reduce the duration mismatch of the traditional life product segment. Justify your answer.

In this case, you would be required to give definitions and explanations of the accrual bonds, making any memorized lists of little value. You could only succeed on this question by having an accurate understanding of the characteristics of accrual bonds. In addition, part (e) of the question requires you to demonstrate an even deeper understanding of the profile of these bonds by evaluating their likely effectiveness in an immunization application. This may not necessarily be an element that was specifically described in the syllabus reading, and therefore, only students who have truly conceptually grasped the material will be able to perform well. In other words, question (e) will separate the students with a truly exceptional understanding (like you!) from those with only surface-level clarity.

It is not always easy to prepare *directly* for explanation questions, due to the large number of fine details that could potentially be tested. If you have adequately learned the material, however, you should feel comfortable that for a question of this type, you will be able to provide a fair number of relevant comments and supporting explanations, as well as a sound rationale for any recommendations made. It is the rationale that will generally be the most important part of the answer.

## 4.3.4  Original Conceptual Question

In addition to a firm grasp of the syllabus material, this question type requires truly original thought and on-the-spot analytical ability. It is without a doubt the hardest type of essay question, and is therefore more common on fellowship exams. The question will present an original problem or situation that is based on elements of the syllabus material, but contain a "twist," requiring you to connect different parts of the syllabus in a meaningful way.

Consider, as an example, the following question taken from another SOA exam. Risk-based capital (RBC) was a topic discussed in several syllabus references for this exam. Though defined slightly differently in each of these references, a general form for a company's RBC is

$$RBC = \sqrt{(C1+C3)^2 + C2^2} + C4,$$

where each "C factor" represents a company's exposure to a given risk. The exam question presented the student with the following *hypothetical* definition of RBC:

$$1.5\sqrt{(C1)^2 + (C3)^2}.$$

It also provided asset portfolio data for a fictitious insurer. It then asked students to comment on the weaknesses of such an RBC formula, to calculate the company's RBC, and to discuss any competitive advantages afforded to the imaginary company under this revised RBC structure. Performing well on this question required a very thorough understanding of issues related to RBC. Many students who learned the RBC formulas from the syllabus and were familiar with their general implementations did not score highly on this question, due to the nature of the independent and "on-the-spot" thinking required.

A subtle point concerning conceptual questions is that, although memorization of a list may not *directly* help you formulate a reply, it might help you to quickly organize your thoughts and consider relevant facts when stating your case. Suppose, for example, that you had memorized a list of the primary desirable characteristics of the RBC formula currently in place. You would be well advised, at least as a starting point, to evaluate the ad-hoc RBC formula given in the question against each of those characteristics. This would demonstrate to the grader, at the very least, that you know and understand those characteristics and are capable of determining whether or not they are present in this particular case. Obviously, however, memorizing lists will not enable you to point out flaws in the formula that do not directly violate a desirable characteristic from the list (and hence this is where the on-the-spot thinking comes into play).

In other words, lists can often serve as useful starting points for evaluation and/or give rise to some issues to consider in preparing your answer. But the only way to thoroughly prepare for original conceptual questions is to take the time to develop a mastery of the syllabus material that extends in depth beyond the norm. Though this can sometimes be a grueling task, resist the temptation to rely entirely on rote memorization of formulas and selected lists of bullet points. It is often the original conceptual questions that have the potential to separate passing candidates from failing candidates.

### 4.3.5 Case Study Questions

Many fellowship examinations will contain questions based on a case study that is distributed in advance (and also during the exam) to all candidates. While the questions pertaining to case studies will not generally be materially different in form from the other questions asked, they will usually require the application of concepts to a realistic situation. I would highly recommend that you become familiar with the case study prior to the exam. Read it several times, and search out senior members of your company to help you gain familiarity with any aspects that you do not understand. It may also be helpful to devise some general ideas regarding questions that could possibly be formed about the case study. I would recommend reviewing past exams for questions pertaining to case studies, and to get others' feedback on features of the case study that seem peculiar, wrong, incomplete, or otherwise interesting.

In the past, many WA examinations contained embedded sections of multiple choice questions. Prior editions of this book contained advice regarding how to best prepare for and answer these kinds of questions, as they often differed in structure from conventional multiple choice questions found on preliminary exams. The use of multiple choice questions on WA examinations has declined in recent years; thus, the advice pertaining to those questions was removed. Some of that content, however, is still relevant to the EA examinations, and accordingly, appears in Section 3.9. To the extent that multiple choice questions are re-introduced to WA examinations in a more prominent manner, I refer the reader to that Section for additional information.

## 4.4   Commercial Study Manuals

Quality commercial study materials for a fellowship exam will contain some or all of the following elements:

1. A detailed outline of the syllabus material, complete with supplementary explanations of difficult concepts and solutions to text exercises (if not already available in published form);

2. A collection of lists, spanning the entirety of the syllabus material and of appropriate depth and length for memorization, often in the form of flashcards;

3. An appreciably large collection of computational problems and other review questions with detailed solutions.

A manual may also contain other miscellaneous elements, such as a study schedule, study tips, replications and/or explanations of text tables and graphs. It should contain adequate space between lines and in the margins to permit you to write notes and comments to supplement the outline given. It should also be typeset in a moderately sized font and be organized in a logical manner that groups related topics together or in "buckets" consistent with the grouping provided by the sponsoring organization for the exam (i.e. SOA or CAS). Many students often find that spiral bound manuals that lie flat on a desk or table are preferable to conventionally bound manuals that are difficult to flatten or have a propensity to close by themselves.

Though the exact importance of good study material in passing a fellowship exam will depend on a student's study style and habits, it is now generally regarded as a necessity. Other additional commercial study aids may also be available, such as sample examinations and CD or DVD recordings, each of which you should evaluate for their appropriateness to your personal situation. Finally, the use of multiple study manuals may also be appropriate for these exams, assuming that the second manual adds incremental value and is not overly repetitive (i.e. it contains additional computational exercises or alternative explanations of difficult syllabus topics).

## 4.5    MISCELLANEOUS SUGGESTIONS

### 4.5.1    Start Early

Many students will find that they can pass preliminary exams with fewer study hours than recommended. Fellowship exams provide a unique challenge to many actuarial students for the following reasons:

1. Studying for fellowship exams requires considerable reading, much of which is devoid of any mathematical equations. Though I do not wish to stereotype, reading comprehension has generally been a weaker area of proficiency for actuarial students. Completing a given section can therefore take considerably more time than you think. This is especially true if you read slowly or generally must read something two or three times to comprehend it fully;

2. There are fewer available computational questions from past exams. This means that you must utilize alternate means to develop an understanding of many of the computational themes for a given exam. It may also mean that you are less sure about the general level of depth and difficulty required on a given exam question;

3. While pursuing fellowship exams, you will probably have assumed more critical responsibilities in the workplace. Often, an untimely work emergency or co-worker illness can cause difficulties in taking study time. As you progress, it generally becomes harder to concentrate on studying for exams to the extent you would like.

In considering all of these factors, it is very important to start studying earlier and more frequently than you initially think is necessary. Though it will vary according to each individual, I found that beginning to study about 2-4 weeks earlier than my study schedule would indicate was generally adequate to cover contingencies but did not cause me to "peak too early."

### 4.5.2 Consolidation

It is critical that separate but related portions of the syllabus be integrated for studying and memorization purposes. Do not blindly rely on a commercial study manual's organization and consolidation of the material! If something makes more sense to you when grouped in a different fashion, then rearrange your notes.

This concept also applies when memorizing lists. If it will aid in your retention, consolidate multiple smaller lists of related content into fewer, larger lists, and reorganize your flashcards to put related material together. This may also help your macro-level conceptual understanding, as grouping of this type can help to clarify a given section's place in the larger context.

### 4.5.3 Study Schedule

I highly recommend that students prepare a study schedule and follow it consistently. While there will certainly be exceptions to this rule, it has been my general observation that 1 hour of study for each minute of an exam is an appropriate lower bound for preparation time. Accordingly, a 5-hour exam will require *at a minimum* 300 hours of study. I intend for this to serve as a lower bound; so while studying more than 350 hours, for example, will not guarantee success, studying less than 300 hours will generally guarantee failure. This is just a general guideline; as you progress through the exam system, you will find the level of required study that suits you individually.

While the number of hours targeted on any given day may vary from student to student, I have generally found it more effective to increase the number of hours studied per day as the exam draws closer. Beginning at a modest level of 1-3 hours per day several months prior to the exam, study time should gradually increase until 4-5 hours or more per day is reached. Obviously, time need not be allocated specifically in these proportions (the weekends can be used to "catch up," for example), but beware of any allocations which are too heavily "back-loaded." Such schedules allow no time for unanticipated interruptions (e.g. illness, work crisis). Also, everyone should develop a self-imposed daily limit, after which studying is no longer effective (this was about 8 hours for me). If you have allocated too many hours on a given day, I urge you to manipulate your schedule until your allocated hours for all days are within your tolerance. Spreadsheet software is excellent for creating a study schedule and tracking hours actually spent studying versus the schedule's requirements. Some commercial study manuals contain study schedules as well, but prior to using them, ensure that they are conducive to your individual style.

Your schedule should allow you to complete the following tasks at least six weeks prior to the exam:

1. Completion of a read-through of all syllabus material, and construction of an outline of the readings (or modification of the outline contained in your study manual);

2. Completion of appropriate end-of-chapter exercises;

3. Completion of a second read-through of difficult portions of the syllabus;

4. Formulation of a complete set of lists for memorization (or modification of the set of lists contained in your study manual(s) or flashcards).

Your last six weeks should be spent doing the following four activities:

1. Memorizing lists;

2. Performing as many computational practice problems as possible;

3.  Continually re-reading your outline of the syllabus material;

4.  Taking sample exams under simulated exam conditions.

Lastly, I wish to emphasize the fact that quality matters over quantity. Using inadequate study tactics or failing to perform appropriate computational problems will likely result in failure, regardless of how many hours you spend studying.

## 4.6    ON EXAM DAY

### 4.6.1   Time Management
For each exam, I advise you to calculate the number of minutes allocated to each point for an exam. If a 5-hour exam contained a total of 100 points, for example, this would translate into three minutes per point. Therefore, you should allocate 15 minutes for a 5-point question, 27 minutes for a 9-point question, and so on.

Be careful to adhere to time limitations when doing a given problem; if you have used your entire time allotment for a given question and cannot finish your answer quickly, I would advise you to move on to the next question and revisit the incomplete questions later as time permits. Timing yourself on each problem is a good way to ensure that you don't jeopardize your chances of success on other questions by spending significantly more time on one question than you have allotted. Many students write the time they began a given question at the top of the page as well as the time at which the allotment will be used, in order to help them keep an appropriate pace throughout the exam.

This approach helps to ensure that you will have at least partially answered all questions rather than over-answered some questions at the expense of others.

### 4.6.2   Answer the Question
Make sure you carefully read the question and construct your answer accordingly. You will receive zero points for your answer, even if it is factually correct, if it does not answer the question

asked. Writing extraneous and irrelevant answers wastes time and does not generate any increase in your score.

If a question asks you to provide a recommendation, do it! Do not just state the pros and cons of each possible course of action; be sure to choose one and defend your choice.

### 4.6.3 The Read-Through Time

Some exams may allow you a short period of reading time prior to commencement. During this period, you will be permitted to read the exam questions but not to write.

Students generally utilize the read-through period in one of two ways:

1. Read all questions on the exam;

2. Find a question that is worth a substantial number of points and contains a large amount of information, and use the time to mentally sort the facts provided and formulate their approach to that question.

I do not recommend (1) since it is unlikely to enhance your performance. Pre-reading a question that you could have already understood during the exam by reading it once or twice amounts to wasted time. Reading a difficult question that is not immediately digested, and then moving on to the next question, also amounts to wasted time, since it has not helped you formulate your answer in any way. In fact, I would argue that the "stress factor" brought on by the knowledge that you have just read a difficult question may actually harm you.

I recommend approach (2). In many cases, beginning a large problem in the wrong way can be a significantly detrimental error if not recognized almost immediately, since it wastes considerable time and does not earn you any points. In fact, in many cases, your performance on a large-point-value question can mean the difference between passing and failing.

### 4.6.4  Lunch

Many upper exams contain a lunch break; it is commonly one hour. Obviously, you will want to use this time to go to the rest room, eat, and, if you are a coffee drinker, grab a cup of java.

Though I personally never did so, I do not necessarily discourage studying during the lunch break. I do however recommend taking the last ten minutes or so of the lunch break to chat with others, relax quietly at your desk, or take a quick walk around the building. Though it is certainly possible that an extra few minutes of studying might help you garner an extra point or two in the event a test question were to focus on the material you happened to be studying, it may just make you more nervous if you discover something you do not understand. And, in either case, having a rested mind and healthy psyche are likely to bolster your performance more than an incremental 10 minutes of study.

If possible, walk to a local luncheon location or bring your lunch from home. Do not risk your exam success by arriving late for the afternoon session due to a traffic accident or other fluke.

### 4.6.5  Writing Your Answers

A fellowship exam requires you to write a significant amount in a very short period of time. You may find, particularly since you likely do far more typing these days than writing, that your hand will begin to ache. For many students (me included), cramping can cause major difficulties in finishing the exam on time.

I recommend bringing multiple pens of different sizes to the exam. When your hand begins to ache, switching to a pen with a different diameter can provide some much needed relief, since it forces the muscles in your hand to grasp the implement in a slightly new manner.

Use blue or black ink pens rather than pencil for WA questions. Be sure to bring several back-ups to ensure that you have enough ink. Concentrate on writing legibly; though this is often difficult when you are in a hurry, writing three additional paragraphs does you no good if none of the graders can read them.

In addition, it would be my advice not to erase or cross out any portions of your written solutions unless they are categorically wrong or conflict with other information in your answer. It is generally true that irrelevant information will not cause you to be penalized so long as it is consistent with the other information you have written, and who knows – it may even earn you a few points! But be sure to avoid making any statements that contradict other portions of your answer.

Finally, resist the temptation to write in complete sentences. Poor grammar and incomplete sentences will not impact your grade so long as they do not compromise the grader's ability to interpret your answer. Write in "bullet" or outline format, and do not waste valuable exam time ensuring that your verb tense is appropriate or doing other miscellaneous structural corrections to your writing! Focus on providing the most information possible in as little time as necessary.

The development of your writing skill is important, but attempting to achieve this on a fellowship exam will not help. Online modules and live courses are better suited for this.

## 4.6.6 Paper

You will be given a pad of lined paper on which to write your answers. Prior to the start of the exam, you will probably notice candidates tearing each sheet off the pad. I recommend you do this as well. This will eliminate the need to later waste valuable exam time separating the sheets, and will avoid creating a disturbance to the other candidates in the test center.

Nobody had ever told me about this, and when I took my first WA exam, I was startled when I observed people all around me simultaneously and frantically tearing paper. I thought it was a protest!

## 4.7   CONCLUSION

The study guidelines presented here provide a strong foundation for preparing for an upper level actuarial exam. You are, however, likely to develop your own unique tactics and put your own personal "spin" on mastering the material and achieving success. In fact, there is probably more room for individuality in studying for fellowship exams than preliminary exams, since the overall preparation procedure is less straightforward. I therefore firmly support individuals wishing to deviate from the techniques provided here, with one caveat. These techniques have been used successfully by many students, and therefore, it should be clear to you, prior to the implementation of any strategy that deviates materially from that described here, that it will in fact enhance your results.

# 5

# GENERAL PREPARATORY GUIDELINES

## 5.1 INTRODUCTION

This chapter was designed to cover the general minutia and extraneous pieces of actuarial exam preparation advice that do not fit naturally under the previous headings or which are not specific to either preliminary or fellowship exams. Some of these are details that I wish someone had shared with me prior to my embarking on the actuarial career path. Others are the result of lessons learned the hard way by colleagues and friends. It is my sincere hope that reading this chapter alleviates you from suffering the same fates, and makes your transition through the actuarial exam cycle as smooth as possible.

## 5.2 MISCELLANEOUS

### 5.2.1 Exam Preparation Seminars

Exam preparation seminars are available from many different vendors. While some are offered in the traditional live classroom or conference room setting, an increasing number are offered via some form of distance education.

Exam-prep seminars have generally proven to be effective for students who have prepared at least moderately well prior to the seminar, and who possess a reasonable familiarity with the material. Seminars usually attempt to bridge the gap between a student's current level of preparedness and the level required for successful completion of an exam. Though their specifics may vary with regard to style, presentation, organization, and quality, most seminars provide a topic-by-topic review of the syllabus material and reinforce that review through the completion of examples, past exam questions, and/or original practice problems.

Live seminars pose several significant advantages to the actuarial student:

1.  They provide an opportunity for students to interact and/or study with other students. In many instances, sharing ideas and solutions with one another and exchanging explanations of difficult syllabus material can be extremely beneficial, especially if other students' approaches to learning particular concepts are uncommon but effective;

2.  They simulate the university classroom environment more closely than most other available methods of instruction. For many working actuarial students, this may represent the most effective educational forum;

3.  They provide an opportunity for the student to ask targeted, specific questions of the instructor in person, as opposed to the electronic medium. For some students, this can enhance understanding and help to clarify ambiguous answers in a more efficient manner;

4.  Seminars tend to cover material in an organized and logical fashion, and may help you integrate related portions of the syllabus material and mentally categorize the subject matter. This is especially important for exams that require that a vast number of reference readings be covered.

Despite the apparent benefits of exam-prep seminars when used as part of a well-rounded study plan, they are generally not an acceptable substitute for traditional self-study. Many underprepared students tend to regard seminars as a "rescue" option, something to make reparations for inconsistent or otherwise ineffectual study habits. Seminars will not generally be a replacement for a traditional, focused study effort over a period of several months, nor will they typically salvage a student who, due to poor or insufficient preparation, is otherwise likely to fail.

When planning to attend a seminar, the following hints will help you gain the most from your experience:

1. Pre-read all of the syllabus material and make an earnest attempt at the appropriate review questions prior to attending;

2. Maintain a list of unanswered questions to bring to the seminar, and ask them during the relevant portion of the instructor's presentation (or at any other appropriate time);

3. Regardless of how tempting it might be, do not skip any assignments the instructor may recommend for completion during the evening (for multi-day seminars). Doing so may compromise the educational integrity of the experience;

4. If you have done many practice problems prior to the seminar, and the seminar instructor hands out original practice problems, it may be advisable to save some of them to ensure the adequate supply of practice problems in the weeks and days immediately preceding the exam.

Distance learning seminars provide a suitable alternative to students that lack the time and/or money to attend a live seminar, or for whom live interaction with an instructor is not crucial to learning. They are usually delivered either over the internet or via pre-recorded lectures. Whether or not a student can derive value from distance learning seminars comparable to that of a live presentation has been the topic of much debate. But before spending the time and money to travel to a live seminar, consider the following advantages afforded by a distance learning seminar:

1. Time that would otherwise be used to travel can now be used to study;

2. For pre-recorded seminars, particularly difficult sections may be revisited at your leisure to ensure understanding;

3. It is sometimes difficult to get the maximum value from a multi-day live seminar which requires intense mental concentration for days at a time;

4. Distance learning seminars are generally less expensive than live seminars and usually do not require you to use valuable company-provided study time;

5. Distance learning seminar instructors are often available via e-mail to answer questions, ensuring that you do not lose out on the question-asking feature.

Distance learning seminars can thus offer many attractive features and deserve to be seriously considered.

## 5.2.2 Self Study vs. Group Study

I generally do not recommend persistent (i.e. more frequently than once weekly) group study, since I have found that it often can result in the waste of valuable study time. I have found, however, that a group that meets periodically to discuss difficult portions of the syllabus and exchange notes, findings, and explanations can greatly enhance performance for all involved. The key is to meet seldom enough that all time spent in the group is quality time and has the potential to impact performance in a positive way. If, however, you are part of a group in which a few students do most of the talking while you (and others) listen, resist the temptation to use the group as a crutch. Inevitably, students who know the material much better than the rest of the group will stop attending, since they will likely feel that their time is not being well spent.

## 5.2.3 Multiple Study Manuals

There is no rule prohibiting students from using more than one study manual. The use of multiple study manuals can be a valuable exam preparation strategy for the following reasons:

1. Different study manuals are likely to employ different methodologies to solve problems, at least for more complicated formulations. The use of multiple study manuals thus increases the likelihood that you will encounter an educational approach that is congruent with your learning style;

2. Different study manuals may contain different computational shortcuts as well as different suggestions for learning to use and memorize those shortcuts;

3. Different study manuals are likely to contain different practice problems, especially if the authors of those study manuals are known to develop original practice problems in addition to relying on recycled questions from past exams (you can never have too many practice problems);

4. Even if a second study manual is rarely used, it may be a valuable resource if referred to in situations in which the presentation of a given topic in the primary study manual is incomplete, incorrect, vague, or simply of poor quality. This is especially true with regard to the more difficult topics on a given exam.

Purchasing one study manual and relying on it exclusively is equivalent to "putting all your eggs in one basket." The notion that a single study manual was written so wonderfully that no other study materials are capable of adding value to your preparation is implausible at best. Of course, there is something to be said for the simplicity afforded by the one-manual approach, but in my opinion, this is easily outweighed by the benefits of a multiple-manual system.

### 5.2.4 Master What Others Skip

Invariably, despite the overwhelming effort put forth by actuarial students and the importance placed on exam success by the profession, many students forego learning some of the material for exams. Though there are many reasons for this, the most common motivation for skipping a section or two is the difficulty level. Students often gamble that a given topic will not appear on the exam, since they feel that the time required to gain a conceptual grasp of that topic might be more effectively spent better learning the remainder of the topics. I have often heard comments such as, *"there is no way that they're going to ask that!"* and *"not even the graders understand that stuff!"* emanating from the study room.

One notable example occurred on a past SOA exam. One particular syllabus reference described a stochastic interest rate model known as the "extended Vasicek trinomial, additive, constant variance model." Associated with this reading was a collection of lengthy, complex formulas. Rather than devote what they thought would be many hours to learning this topic, some students decided to "roll the dice," hoping that this material would not serve as the subject of an exam question. Many of them were disappointed to find not only that question 4 on this exam was a written answer question devoted to this topic, but that it was worth a whopping 9 points, making it the largest point-valued question on the exam and significantly reducing the chances of passing for anyone that skipped this material.

I firmly advocate learning very well what others decide to skip. Nearly everyone will be equipped to answer more manageable questions; it is by performing well on questions that others have answered poorly that you will succeed in setting yourself apart from the pack. Furthermore, since it is almost always the case that material is skipped because it is lengthy and difficult, it is reasonable to assume that any exam questions related to this material would be long and difficult, and therefore worth more points. I therefore strongly advise you not to skip material, and to learn especially well the material that is skipped by others.

### 5.2.5  Calculator Use

Section 3.5 discussed the importance of developing suitable calculator proficiency for preliminary exams. There are also some general guidelines for calculator use that apply across all types of examinations:

1.  Do all practice problems during the study phase with the same calculator that you will use for the exam. This will help to ensure that you are sufficiently familiar with the location of the various buttons on the calculator, and that you can utilize memory keys effectively. Follow the suggestions of Section 3.5, or consult the instruction manual, to ensure that you are fully aware of and proficient in using all of the relevant features and functions of your calculator;

2.  Be sure that the calculator you are using is listed as an approved calculator for the exam you are taking. Consult the website of the sponsoring organization of the exam for a list of approved calculators.

## 5.3   The Night Before The Exam

### ►Pack Your Bags!

The evening before the exam, gather everything you will need to bring the following day and place it together. This includes:

1.  Your examination admission ticket;

2.  Acceptable sources of identification;

3.  A watch;

4.  Writing implements (for a preliminary exam, at least five pencils with appropriate lead and erasers, and for a fellowship exam, at least four pens of varying diameters, with blue or black ink, as well as three pencils for any MC sections);

5.  Two calculators (be sure your calculators are listed among the acceptable models), at least one of which is battery-powered;

6.  Any snacks you may want to eat prior to the exam or during intermission (if applicable);

7.  A bottle of water or other permitted beverage for use during the exam;

8.  Any medication you will need;

9.  Any items specifically required by examination centers administering exams via CBT;

10. Any other miscellaneous (but permissible) items you wish to bring.

Do not wait until the morning to gather the required items. This is an unnecessary risk that takes only minutes to eliminate the evening before an exam.

## ▶ Petrol

If driving to the exam, be sure your vehicle has an appropriate amount of gasoline to enable you to get to the test center without stopping for a refill. A colleague (who left for the exam inexcusably late) once ran short on gas, and was forced to spend his valuable read-through time at the pumps!

## ▶ Snooze, Anyone?

Though it might be difficult, try to get the amount of sleep you would ordinarily need to feel rested. For most of us, this is around seven hours. Also, do not go to bed uncharacteristically early; this may cause grogginess.

Program at least two alarms to make sure you don't oversleep. I admit that due to nerves, this is hardly a risk for many people (including me). You may want to make sure that at least one of these alarms is battery-powered, just to guard against the unlikely event that an overnight power outage prevents the other from performing its duty.

## ▶ Studying

Studying the evening before the exam is a matter of personal taste. I used the night before the exam to get everything ready, as I described earlier, and then rested my brain by engaging in some relaxing activity, such as television or dinner out. I always found that the benefits afforded by relaxing my mind far outweighed the very few incremental points that an extra hour or two of studying could potentially allow me to earn. This was particularly true since nervousness usually precluded me from deriving full value from last-ditch studying anyway.

Many people, however, find that they are driven by anxiety to study the evening before the exam. If you find that you simply cannot relax, then it is probably acceptable to do *some* studying. But beware – several studies have shown that a relaxation period just prior to intense mental exercise tends to enhance performance.

Just take it easy, and by all means, make sure you don't sacrifice valuable hours of sleep in a late night study binge!

### ▶ Where in the World Am I Going?

If you have any doubts about your ability to locate the test center, take a road trip the evening before the exam, and take detailed notes about how to get there. Do not rely on your memory unless you are absolutely sure what route to take.

In addition, I would caution you against unconditionally relying on directions from another person, a GPS system, or an internet navigation site. There is always the potential for error.

## 5.4   ON EXAM DAY

### ▶ Bring a Sweater!

At the risk of sounding like your mother, I urge you to dress in layers for the exam. Temperature control can vary significantly from one test center to the next. It is therefore very useful to dress in layers, allowing you to adjust your body temperature and maintain your physical comfort, which, in turn, will maximize your potential.

### ▶ Leave Early from Home

Though it would seem fairly obvious, you would be surprised at how many times I have observed latecomers at actuarial exams. Not only do they hamper their own chances of passing by arriving late, they disturb all other exam candidates in the process. Therefore, as a courtesy to yourself and to others, refrain from sleeping in, procrastinating, and leaving too late for the exam.

When determining how early it is necessary to leave to arrive on time, assume that you will be driving at the speed limit! One colleague departed from home for an exam at his planned time, leaving what he thought was "plenty of time." It was only adequate time for *him*, if all goes according to plan, since he usually drives at the speed of light! He arrived late to the exam after spending 10 minutes in the shoulder of the interstate pleading innocence to a state police officer, who, unaware of what an actuary is or what actuaries do, did not have very much sympathy for him!

Also, be sure to add time to your estimate to account for traffic conditions, inclement weather, and other contingencies.

## ▶ Travel in Packs

When traveling to an exam, make plans to meet at least one other party in the morning, and drive to the exam in separate vehicles but within close proximity. This can be viewed as a contingency, in the unlikely event that one party experiences car trouble, is involved in an accident, or suffers some other misfortune. Of course, if you rear-end your fellow travel companions, then you are both out of luck!

## ▶ Tunes

En route to the exam, listen to something inspirational. What qualifies as inspirational is obviously a very personal matter, so I urge you to follow your heart. Some prefer something relaxing, such as classical music or talk radio. Others may enjoy the silence. Personally, I favored loud, aggressive music that put me into a competitive mood (for the sake of professionalism, I will not cite the exact artists). Go with whatever you feel will enhance your performance.

## ▶ Carefully Plan Meals and Restroom Usage

Avoid foods with objectionable digestive consequences on, and the night before, exam day. If possible, appropriately time your exam-day meals, particularly your fluid intake, to reduce the probability of bathroom visitation. Use the restroom as late as possible before the exam begins. Spending exam time in the bathroom is like going to the concession stand in the middle of the most important scene in a great movie, or standing in line for a snack while the winning touchdown is being scored.

I know a talented exam taker whose only failure was due to an incident in which he ate a particularly spicy food prior to the exam. Try as he might to delay the inevitable, he was forced to spend 10 minutes of a 90-minute examination in the bathroom, and finished only 18 of the 20 questions on the exam. He guessed on the remaining two questions, which he could have easily solved with another five minutes, and failed with a 5.

## ► Follow the Directions Carefully

Though it is sometimes difficult to concentrate on the proctor while awaiting the start of an exam, be sure to carefully follow all directions given. If applicable, sign your test booklet and answer envelope – if you forget, your exam will not be graded! For fellowship exams, be sure your candidate number appears on each answer page. Stop writing when told by the proctor that time has expired. You get the idea. Following directions carefully will help to ensure that there are no difficulties in grading your exam and no confusion as to any dishonest actions on your part.

## ► Do Not Cheat

While this section will not prove to be necessary for most of you, I do recognize, since I have witnessed acts of dishonesty during actuarial exams, that a handful of you may spend your study hours dreaming up ingenious methods to cheat on the exams. I will not divulge any of the countless propositions to which I have been exposed, for fear that they might provide some of you with mental ammunition. It suffices to say that a wide variety of strategies have surfaced, most unsuccessfully.

Besides the obvious moral argument against cheating, which is likely adequate to discourage the vast majority of you from perpetrating, I have some factors to consider for those of you left over:

1. Anecdotally, cheaters are rarely successful (both in cheating and in passing the exam);

2. The penalties for cheating, if caught, are very severe and will most certainly outweigh any benefits previously obtained by cheating;

3. Colleagues will often "catch on" to cheaters, even if they are successful in covering their tracks from the proctor. Fellow students often report cheaters to SOA, but even if they do not, the cheaters' professional rapport will be irreversibly damaged, making future career success unlikely. This is particularly true in the "small circle" that is actuarial science.

I heavily discourage even the smallest forms of cheating; it is simply not worth the risk.

Both the SOA and CAS have published guidelines pertaining to ethical conduct. The SOA's Code of Professional Conduct has 14 precepts that set forth what it means for an actuary to act as a professional, and identifies the responsibilities that actuaries have to the public, to their clients and employers, and to the actuarial profession. The Code has been formally adopted by the AAA, SOA, CAS, ASPPA, and CAA, and can be found on the SOA website.

In addition, in 2006, the CAS developed a "Code of Professional Ethics for Candidates," in recognition of the fact that CAS candidates, prior to becoming members of the CAS, often perform responsible actuarial work but were not bound by a professional code. All candidates registering for CAS–specific Exams 3L and 5–9 must sign a statement that they have read the Code and agree to be bound by it. The SOA has a similar code, entitled "Code of Conduct for Candidates," which was adopted in 2008.

I would encourage aspiring actuaries to periodically review the relevant Code. Joining the actuarial profession is a privilege, and it is up to all its current and prospective members to guard its integrity.

## ►Keep it in Perspective

My last piece of advice for exam day is to keep the exam, and the exam process, in perspective. You may find that despite countless study hours and enormous personal sacrifices, and despite following all of the advice in this book and in others, you simply do not perform well on an exam. You may walk out of the test center in a daze. Situations such as these have the potential to cause depression, anxiety, and other severe reactions if they are not viewed in the appropriate light. It is not easy for anyone, let alone aspiring actuaries, to handle failure.

Keep your head up, and move on with life! Once the test is out of your hands, and into those of the proctor, you are powerless to change your answers or your performance. So, resist the temptation to obsess over every question and how your answer might fare, and try not to talk about the exam in your spare time. Instead, forget about the exam and focus on having some fun, at least for a month or two, until it is time to order those books and dig in once again!

## 5.5 SUPERSTITION

Though it would usually be regarded as unorthodox to devote a section of a book on proper study habits to the perpetuation of superstitions, I wish to provide you with an inside glimpse at the cultural dynamics that have grown out of the grueling actuarial exam system. Students cope with the stress and pressure created by exams in very diverse ways. Some become ritualistic in their behavior, feeling that "getting into a groove" is the best way to maintain momentum in the long run. Others find repetition monotonous, and do all they can to "mix it up" to cope with the daily realities of studying actuarial science. Still others seem to vacillate between these extremes, prone to the occasional compulsive behavior but trying to change their routine and have a little fun. Whatever the case, one thing is for sure; these wide variations have created some strange behavior, and some very funny stories, a few of which I will share.

I myself fell victim to this compulsion; in fact, I suffered from a particularly strong manifestation. My irrationalities began with my second exam. Having done very well on my first exam, and wishing to duplicate this on the second exam, I wore the same clothes (including socks and underwear – don't worry, they had been laundered), and took the exam in the same chair. After doing very well on the second exam, the ritual was firmly ingrained, and I became convinced that altering anything about my exam-day habits would lead to failure. In fact, I also began to drink the same size and flavor of coffee, read the same section of the newspaper, and even eat the same muffin for breakfast.

I also carried a relatively unconventional habit from my youth into my exam-taking days. As a youngster, my father would always give me a tablespoon full of honey the morning of an exam to provide me with a little "kick" of exam-day energy. He maintained that honey's gelatinous texture would prevent the body from processing it too quickly, causing a strategically timed energy burst precisely at the moment it is needed the most – two or three hours into an exam! I carried this habit into adulthood, gobbling a tablespoon full of honey the morning of each actuarial exam. Though I was sure that my father's recommendation was nothing more than an old-world superstition, I found myself unable to break away.

While registering for my first Fellowship examination, I had a troubling realization. Since the University of Connecticut was an official test site only for certain preliminary exams, I would be forced to discontinue my ritual of sitting at the same table, in the same chair, for every exam. Nervous, and unsure of myself, I traveled to an unfamiliar test center to take the exam, where I was flustered by my new surroundings and disappointed in the lack of table space. To compound matters, I realized that I had accidentally left my watch at home on the kitchen table!

After glancing around the room and failing to observe a clock, I rushed outside to try to find a local vendor. However, it was 7:30 in the morning, and given that this particular test center was not located in what you could realistically call a thriving business community, I had my doubts. I roamed a few blocks in search of a jeweler. After walking a considerable distance, I finally stumbled upon a pawnbroker, where I tried to purchase the only watch in the store – what appeared to be a "previously owned" Rolex. Unfortunately, the price of $495 was slightly more than I was able to pay at the time. I called my then-girlfriend (now my wife), who drove to my apartment, retrieved my watch, drove to the test center in her pajamas, and delivered my watch to me on the corner adjacent to the test center with only minutes to spare. By the time I ran upstairs, I had just enough time to settle down, stop sweating, have a drink of water, and get to my seat. Ah, life on the edge as an actuary!

The irony of the story surfaced when, only a minute or two later, a proctor entered the room carrying a large wall clock, which she promptly mounted about eight feet from my desk. Fortunately, despite this odd set of circumstances, I passed the exam, but many of my co-workers got a good laugh from this incident for a long time afterward!

I have also witnessed other forms of ritualistic behavior. Though the primary method for disseminating the passing candidate numbers for actuarial exams has become the internet, a paper copy verifying the score is sent by regular mail to all candidates. A colleague of mine had passed several exams consecutively, and was feeling confident about another that he had recently taken. It would be the first exam for which candidates could check their exam results online. After logging on and failing to observe his candidate number on the pass list, he vowed to never again utilize the internet to check his score. In fact, for each of his subsequent exams, he waited for the paper score report to discover his fate. To others, this was pure insanity! After all, it is difficult enough to wait the 10 or so weeks until grades are posted that nerve-wracking Friday afternoon, let alone to spend an additional three days in the dark unnecessarily. But for this student, whose superstitions overrode any rational thoughts about the impact upon his performance of his means of determining results, doing anything other than waiting for the mailer was lunacy.

One colleague of mine insisted on using a brand new set of pens for each examination. She maintained that an old pen "had written something incorrect at some point in its life," and was therefore "irreversibly scarred." Another never studied without a beer, and to ensure that his study environment closely simulated that of the test center, would drink a beer prior to the exam as well (I do not recommend this)!

Though I admittedly possess only a very rudimentary under-standing of psychology, I can state confidently from my own experiences that the mind, though powerful and complex, can also be extremely frail. Therefore, if you find yourself developing *reasonably insignificant* superstitions, indulge them! This compel-ling and highly personalized exam weaponry, whether real or imagined, can help all of us find comfort during some of the most stressful times in our lives. As odd as it might sound to others, I truly felt that swallowing honey and wearing my old hat and baggy jeans gave me an edge that other candidates did not have, and regardless of the degree of rationality of this emotion, it made me more confident, eased my nerves, and ultimately, bolstered my performance.

## 5.6   CONCLUSION

I have presented sound exam preparation advice from which all students can benefit. There are other miscellaneous sources devoted to helping students prepare for actuarial exams, nearly all of which contain some subset of the material in this book. Nonetheless, I encourage you to consult additional resources at your discretion. The CAS offers a newsletter for candidates entitled "Future Fellows." All past issues can be found at www.casact.org/newsletter/index.cfm?fa=ffmain. In addition, the Education section of the SOA contains a great deal of information on exam-related issues, including tips for studying for and taking exams, and the methodology used for determining the pass mark. It may be found at www.soa.org. Of course, consulting fellow students, especially those with a proven track record for success, can be a great way to learn more.

# 6

# Today's Advice For Tomorrow's Actuaries

## 6.1 Introduction

Thus far, this book has focused almost exclusively on aiding you in your arduous journey through the actuarial credentialing process. Due to the tremendous aptitude and commitment required by this endeavor, the importance of a credential to advancement as an actuary, and the credibility and prestige assigned to professional actuarial credentials, it is easy to regard the completion of this process as the "top of the mountain." Though the sound analytical skill and mathematical proficiency required for the successful achievement of an actuarial credential have long been the hallmark of the actuary, possessing these traits in isolation is rarely sufficient for a truly successful career. As the range of potential roles played by actuaries in the workplace evolves, employers are demanding more from their actuaries, as they should.

This may come as shock to many, particularly those whose idea of a day in the life of an actuary is based upon antiquated notions of actuaries performing longhand calculations to construct tables of survival probabilities and annuity discount factors. Today, computers do this work, leaving the actuary with many more interesting (and challenging) duties. Perhaps an analogy to medicine will crystallize the point.

Suppose you were to contract an illness, and travel to the doctor's office for treatment. You would likely have several baseline expectations for your visit, including the following:

1.  You would expect your doctor to be accepted by the medical community, to refrain from inappropriately slandering other medical professionals, and to refer you to a specialist if your illness was outside the realm of her expertise;

2.  You would expect your doctor to know the medical business; that is, to be able to diagnose your illness accurately, to identify and understand the urgency of an appropriate treatment regimen, and to make use of the best available resources in scheduling timely and effective treatment;

3.  You would expect that upon diagnosing you, your doctor would be able to explain your illness to you, as well as the recommended treatment plan, in terms you could understand;

4.  You would expect your doctor to have properly trained her office personnel, so that they handle your files professionally, call your prescriptions in as promised, and keep an accurate log of your appointments and payments;

5.  You would expect your doctor to be able to relate to you in a courteous and respectful manner;

6.  You would expect your doctor to have remained knowledge-able of any new developments and emerging diseases in medicine, so that if your illness happened to be a fairly new manifestation, she would be able to accurately diagnose you.

Though clearly practicing an entirely different discipline, these expectations are analogous to those that apply to actuaries. In this chapter, I will provide some general commentary on issues that you should be considering as you put together your actuarial career plans. First, I will touch briefly on some of the cultural aspects of companies and actuarial student programs. I will then discuss, at a very basic level, some elements of your repertoire that you will want to focus on over the course of your career, all of which will impact your career success, for better or for worse. These elements include communication skills, leadership skills, ongoing professional education, and business acumen. Obviously these topics are very broad, and a comprehensive treatment of each would be well beyond the scope of this book. Instead, it is my aim to reiterate the importance of each from a career development standpoint, and to provide some basic resources and suggestions that you can use to independently further your progress in these areas.

## 6.2    CULTURE AND COMPETITIVENESS

Actuarial employers come in all shapes and sizes, and actuarial students will find that there can be pros and cons to each. While I am obviously unable to describe the nuances of specific cultural differences that distinguish various companies from one another, I am prepared to offer some anecdotal evidence on the major dimensions of variation. My hope is that this brief discussion triggers some active thought about the types of employers for whom you may wish to be employed as well as the cultural elements that are important to you in a work environment.

Employers can sometimes have very different visions regarding the extent to which the contributions of individuals should be recognized in relation to those of the teams for which they work. Some companies choose to predominantly recognize and reward team performance, rather than single out specific team members. This may also mean that individual compensation arrangements tend to be comprised of many components that are determined on the basis of the team's success in attaining its objectives. On the other hand, some companies heavily recognize individual performance to the exclusion of the team's overall success or failure. In extreme cases, individual performance measures are publicized to the entire workforce, and competition between coworkers is not only a natural consequence but sometimes a direct managerial objective. Correspondingly, compensation may also be based heavily upon management's perception of your performance or some other "objective" metric of your productivity. Many workers are capable of handling even very competitive environments with professionalism and moral soundness. While I would be reluctant to say that environments such as these *create* significant barriers to healthy office culture, I do feel that they are dangerous breeding grounds for those already predisposed to self-serving or faithless behavior. I will present an unfortunate example of this a bit later.

Most employers probably fall comfortably in the middle of these two extremes; but even so, a slight predilection for one over the other is likely. Your personality will largely dictate the extent to which you like or dislike individual competition at work. Many find that the constant pressure of being compared with peers keeps them motivated and bolsters their performance, while others are rattled by intra-office pressures and fail to perform in relation to their potential.

There is also significant variation with respect to employers' views on employee development. Some companies deliberately and frequently rotate employees through various roles within and among various lines of business, including those with which the employees have no experience or expertise. This development model provides actuaries with the opportunity to acquire a broad array of skills, a fundamental knowledge base of multiple markets in the industry, and a sense for the company's overall business posture.

Other companies are more likely to grow their future business leaders from within specific lines of business; that is, actuaries begin their careers in a specific line and gradually progress through its ranks as their expertise grows.

The degree to which you may favor one of these paradigms over another will again largely depend upon your personality and career aspirations. Rotating frequently within a given company will provide you with broad-based experiences and a diverse skill set, possibly at the expense of a superior degree of specialization in any one marketplace. This will be particularly attractive to you if you enjoy learning new things and if your eyes are set on an organizational leadership position that involves oversight of multiple company functions. Progressing in a single function or line of business, on the other hand, will prove attractive to you if you wish to develop a considerably specialized focus in one marketplace or practice area. This can prove very advantageous if the chosen area is emerging in popularity and/or importance. It may, however, mean that your development of overall business knowledge and competencies will suffer.

There are many other dimensions of variation between companies that impact culture. Listed below, in no particular order, are *some* of the most culturally influential factors in modern business environments:

- The type of company (single-line vs. multi-line);

- Corporate ownership;

- The size of the company;

- The industry in which the company competes (insurance, consulting, financial services, government, etc);

- The length of time that the company has been in business;

- The company's compensation and incentive programs;

- Company management's focus and expertise in building comradeship and morale;

- The company's success in its business endeavors.

Apart from company-wide culture, there are some additional social considerations associated specifically with actuarial student programs. Inevitably, the existence of such programs within a corporate environment creates competition. In many companies, whether right or wrong, salary increases, promotions, and professional status for actuaries are heavily influenced by relative exam success. In some companies, there are unwritten (but culturally clearly defined) performance standards, as well as subtle interstudent competitive pressures, that can negatively impact your nerves, your attitude toward your work, and your view of your employer and colleagues. In more severe cases, company senior management believes that deliberately fostering antagonistic competition between actuarial students enhances exam performance. Some students may thrive in this environment, while others may struggle.

It is also important to note that the behavior of individual participants in actuarial training programs may create problematic cultural conditions independent of the program structure or management's philosophy. I have heard about some truly despicable actions during my career. One incident I can recall relates to a study group formed at a friend's company by five students with the goal of aiding in the preparation for a certain exam. On the exam syllabus was a particularly difficult topic that none of the students was able to grasp. As time went by, the students became progressively more worried about their lack of understanding of this material, and were searching out more knowledgeable individuals that might be able to lend a helping hand. The students were able to procure some moderately helpful answers to their questions, and though not overly confident in their insights, did feel a bit more comfortable.

On the day of the actual exam, the students encountered what they had feared the most; the largest question on the exam focused specifically on this particular topic, and was posed with such granularity that it was doubtful that any of them could answer it well. Due to having roughly the same knowledge base as a result of studying together in groups, the students performed at roughly the same level on the exam; two of these students scored 5's and two scored 6's. The last member, however, conspicuously scored a 9. It was later discovered that this student had acquired a great deal of knowledge regarding the relevant topic from an external source and deliberately withheld it from the rest of the group, hoping to increase his chances of passing by sandbagging his colleagues. Needless to say, this student had severely and permanently damaged his future working relationships with his fellow students.

As the above example would suggest, knowing how to respond to many of the nuances of varying student program climates can be challenging. I am prepared to offer the following suggestions for functioning within an actuarial training program:

1. Never knowingly withhold information, books, notes, flash-cards, or study tips from other students in the program from which they could benefit. In fact, volunteer such items. Be an "open book" about what you have to offer. Not only will you

sleep better, but this trend will likely earn you a great deal of personal respect and professional admiration. This far outweighs any of the perceived benefits of denying others, even in the extraordinarily unlikely case that it actually were to make the difference between passing and failing an exam;

2. If you pass an exam, do not tell anyone unless they ask. A comment of this type can easily be construed as a gloat, even if it was not intended to be. This is especially true around results time, as emotions are high and sensitivities are likely to be greater. Furthermore, a reputation for pompousness is very difficult to shake;

3. If you fail an exam, hold your head up high and congratulate those who pass. This will not only strengthen your working relationships but will build your reputation as a composed and unpretentious person who is capable of dealing with setbacks (often a quality evidenced in successful senior managers!).

Since individuals are motivated in unique ways, and some will find varying types of employer environments more conducive to their personal styles than others, I will refrain from making any recommendations regarding what I feel to be the most desirable characteristics of an employer; after all, they are highly relative. I will encourage you, however, prior to accepting or rejecting any offer of employment, to make an objective assessment of the working environment into which you have been invited. Consider the prospective employer with regard to the elements discussed here, as well as with respect to other factors that you personally deem important. Asking those with diverse employment experiences can be a valuable way to gain insight; just remember that you are the one that must ultimately be satisfied with the decision. Though salary differentials between two or more competing offers can potentially impact your objectivity, resist the temptation to necessarily accept the best-paying offer. In my opinion, you are likely to execute better when you are happy, which will lead to better job performance, and therefore, greater monetary rewards in the long run.

## 6.3    COMMUNICATION SKILLS

Effective written and oral communication skills have not generally been the trademark of most actuaries. A few reasons for this follow:

1.  An actuary's college or university curriculum is focused heavily on mathematical, statistical, and business fundamentals, and therefore does not generally provide the training and practice required for building communication skills;

2.  An actuary in the beginning stages of her career may find that the vast majority of her job functions require technical competency only. Therefore, despite practicing in a professional arena, the development of communication skills may be impeded by basic time constraints and job/exam pressures;

3.  Actuarial exams have tended not to focus on building these skills. Even written answer exams, despite the images of essay writing that their title suggests, do not reward effective written communication. While it is certainly true that abysmal writing skills will make it more difficult for you to succeed on these exams, this hardly implies that preparing for exams will *improve* your communication skills. While recent changes in the education system have begun to address this issue, it is doubtful that this initiative, in isolation, will do much to rectify the situation;

4.  A large number of actuaries practice in a language other than their native tongue. While the range of proficiency in the second language varies widely, and while many have managed to develop language skills comparable to native speakers, there remain those whose language competency lags behind.

Prior to the advent of computers, actuaries spent virtually all of their time calculating premiums and reserves by hand. The resulting stereotypes of actuaries are not very flattering, and we have all heard the jokes. Today's business environment, however, demands that actuaries become involved in many cross-sectional activities of a company's daily operations. This new paradigm creates a far more interesting work environment for today's actuaries. It also creates a greater need for effective oral and written communication skills. In fact, failing to develop your communication skills will be a significant roadblock to future career success. Examples of applications follow:

1.  Increasingly, actuaries are called upon to formulate legal strategy, review documentation and prospectuses, and complete required regulatory filings. They will frequently be involved in negotiations with regulators;

2.  Actuaries are often responsible for briefing senior management, many of whom do not have an actuarial background, on important quantitative advances and risk management strategies. Due to the growing complexity of such initiatives, actuaries are challenged more now than ever to explain the pros and cons of various options, secure buy-in from management, and ensure proper execution;

3.  Most actuaries must interact often with a variety of technical and non-technical audiences, including underwriters, captive agents, regulators and ratings agencies, lawyers, sales personnel, financial analysts, accountants, investment professionals, and a multitude of other constituencies;

4.  As actuaries grow in their careers, they may be responsible for teams of employees that include non-actuaries, further increasing the importance of giving and accepting feedback and providing unambiguous directives to staff.

Probably the most prominent communication barrier in the actuarial community is the tendency of actuaries to be too technical when conveying ideas to others. This is significantly problematic if senior managers have non-technical backgrounds. Conversations can quickly become frustrating for both parties. Here is an example:

*Actuary*: "Thank you for meeting with me today. As you know, our variable annuity products have some very aggressive equity guarantees, and I wanted to meet with you to discuss some ways we might possibly mitigate our risk."

*Senior Manager*: "No problem. Let's hear your proposal."

*Actuary*: "Well, the VA products have guaranteed minimum death benefits. These are basically embedded put options on the index which ...."

*Senior Manager*: "Embedded what?"

*Actuary*: "Put options ... you know, it pays off if the underlying asset is less than the strike price ... like in the death benefit case, if the index value falls, the policyholder's benefit is in the money and..."

*Senior Manager*: "In the money? Who is in the money? I thought we were in the money from selling these products."

*Actuary*: "No, 'in the money' is an expression; it means that the benefit's value exceeds the value of the policyholder's account. So we set up a hedge. The strategy is essentially to dynamically replicate the put option we've sold, by maintaining delta-neutrality in the underlying, so we are immunized against ..."

*Senior Manager*: "Whoa, whoa, whoa. Slow down. I need plain English here. Dynamically replicating, alpha-neutral, hullabaloo."

*Actuary*: "Um, well, it's like this. We get some assets that make money if the index goes down. That way, if the index drops and our policies begin to ..."

*Senior Manager*: "So it pays the claims for us if the market goes down?"

*Actuary*: "That's right."

*Senior Manager*: "OK. What happens if the market goes up?"

*Actuary*: "Well, then we lose money. But we don't care, since we won't have to pay the claims on the death benefit."

*Senior Manager*: "Of course we care. That's like saying that we don't care if sales fall in Great Britain since they're up in America. We are still losing money, aren't we? How is this risk management? I thought the goal of risk management was to avoid losses."

As the example points out, technical conversations between actuaries and senior managers can prove difficult to navigate. The impediments created by technical conversation are not limited to one-on-one interactions or small meetings. In many cases, actuaries must make presentations to groups of individuals from various backgrounds, in order to discuss recent product innovations, risk management initiatives, or other projects. Many actuaries quickly develop a reputation for making highly technical (and often unintelligible) presentations. In my experience, this is usually due to one of the following two reasons:

1. They may believe that presenting ideas very technically will make them immune to criticism (since the other parties to the conversation lack the expertise to refute anything that is said);

2. They may believe that an extremely technical presentation will so impress the audience that any proposals will be accepted without question.

This practice has several unfavorable consequences:

1. It causes others to regard you as arrogant, and in the long run, ruins your potential as a leader in the eyes of others;

2. It causes others to perceive you as narrow-minded, i.e., unable to conceptualize the "larger picture;"

3. If senior managers feel that communicating with you is labor-intensive, they will circumvent you when seeking answers; this

not only reduces your visibility but creates a "glass ceiling" for you and your career.

Developing technical communication competency is critical to ongoing success in your career; after all, regardless of how good your ideas are, they are worthless if others cannot understand the value they can add to the organization.

While general suggestions for improving communication skills will be given later in the chapter, the following are some specific suggestions to aid in the development of your ability to explain technical concepts to others:

1.  While in college, get a job tutoring lower-level math courses. In this capacity, you will interact with people whose career focuses are completely devoid of math. In many cases, their only goal may be to pass the math course to satisfy a requirement, and move on to the rest of their courses. This is a perfect opportunity to practice explaining technical concepts to non-technical people, or at the very least, to people whose interest does not extend to technical realms. Those of you having already graduated from college could obtain similar experience by tutoring at your local public high school;

2.  Rather than shy away from helping co-workers with technical projects, engage these situations as teaching opportunities;

3.  Buy and read a few books on the subject. Though a search on an Internet bookstore will reveal scores of matches, one such book with a good reputation is *Effective Communication Skills for Scientific and Technical Professionals*, by Harry Chambers.

Another factor contributing to communication difficulties is the compensation structure of many corporate organizations, which motivates employees to work toward competing objectives. In many cases, actuaries are unfortunately thrust into the middle of difficult decisions created by this phenomenon. For example, the sales manager may wish to increase commissions or make product changes that are more favorable to the client, since these actions will increase sales. Such changes generally make the product less profitable from a corporate standpoint. The actuaries in the given line of business must strike a balance between implementing changes that satisfy the sales personnel but maintain appropriate product profitability. Such situations often make effective communication very difficult, due to the emotional sensitivity involved. An (admittedly stylized) example follows:

*Sales*: "Fixed annuities are hot right now. If we offer a crediting rate of 7% on new money, we could easily sell tons of business."

*Actuary*: "Assuming we don't want to take on any more credit risk in the asset portfolio then offering a 7% rate on new money will drop our net spread substantially and bring this product to a 3% IRR. So, you see, supporting this rate is not possible under any circumstances. We just can't afford it."
*Sales*: "What is an IRR?"

*Actuary*: "It's the rate of return on the investment. So in this case, my model indicates that if we were to implement your crediting rate suggestion, that we could expect a 3% return on any business we were to sell."

*Sales*: "But if we get a 3% IRR, we are still making money. It makes no sense to refuse to sell profitable business! Aren't you supposed to be a math expert?"

*Actuary*: "That would only be true if we had unlimited capital. But efficient capital allocation is necessary to ensure that we have positive growth in shareholder economic value."

*Sales*: "What are you talking about? And, anyway, if that is true, why can other companies afford these rates, but we can't?"

*Actuary*: "Other companies may have different profit targets, different policyholder behavior assumptions, or different ..."

*Sales*: "So why can't we adjust our profit targets, or our policyholder behavior assumptions? Then it isn't an issue."

*Actuary*: "But you just can't move the model assumptions around whenever you want."

*Sales*: "What's the alternative? Not sell any business?"

*Actuary*: "No business may be better than bad business."

*Sales*: "Says who? How am I supposed to hit my sales targets with bad products? Maybe it's better for YOU. But it's not better for ME; you are tying my hands."

*Actuary*: "How am I supposed to hit my profitability targets if the only products you can sell are bad for the company?"

*Sales*: "Keep it up. Then we won't sell any business, and we'll all be out of a job."

This is just one example of the types of difficult dialogue that actuaries are faced with in the course of their duties. It suffices to say that all actuaries will be forced to traverse such rough terrain in their careers, and should focus early on building appropriate competencies. While many more specific suggestions will be available through the resources provided at the end of this section, some fundamental guidelines for communicating in difficult situations follow:

1.  Listen

    Be sure you listen to what other people are saying, especially if you think that you may later advance an opposing point of view. Though this seems obvious, it is more difficult than it appears, especially when emotional sensitivity is high – people are less effective communicators when under pressure. Perhaps one of the worst communication errors that can be made is formulating one's response mentally while another participant is speaking; this causes you to miss the entirety of what is being said and presumes (quite arrogantly) that nothing being said can possibly impact your point of view.

2.  Reflect

    After thoroughly listening, reflect what you have heard back to
    the other person. This dramatically reduces communication
    errors, prevents participants from spending time debating a
    point that was never made (which happens with an alarmingly
    high frequency), and ensures that all critical information has
    been successfully relayed. Phrases such as "What I hear you
    saying is ..." and "If I understand correctly, ..." are
    astoundingly valuable.

3.  Validate

    Validate the views and concerns of others, especially if you
    disagree with their content. This will generally make it easier
    for others to accept your input. Additionally, and perhaps most
    importantly, it will subtly emphasize the fact that reasonable
    people can disagree, thereby allowing others to remain
    unthreatened and non-defensive within a group setting.

4.  Respond

    Take careful note; "respond" is the fourth item on the list. A
    surefire way to stunt your career is to make it the first. You
    should only respond with your own view after you have
    thoroughly listened to others, confirmed your understanding,
    and provided sincere validation.

5.  Bridge the gap

    Using the above guidelines, always attempt to bridge the gap
    between the interests of various stakeholders when posing a
    solution, keeping the best interest of the organization in mind.
    In a majority of cases it is possible for everyone to win. In
    some situations, however, such as when two groups are
    absolutely diametrically opposed, this will not be possible, and
    difficult decisions must be made after considering all factors.

I have just three other miscellaneous pieces of advice to keep in mind
while executing the above steps:

1.  Give others the benefit of the doubt. If you are interacting with someone who you know to be competent, but who appears to be advocating an illogical point of view, never "jump the gun." There is often more to a situation or viewpoint than you initially perceive. It is likely that either he poorly communicated his motivations, that he failed to share some information that would "tie things together," or that you have done a poor job listening. His position will likely seem far more reasonable after some additional dialogue and reflexive listening. Of course it is entirely possible that his judgment is "off the mark" in this particular situation, but by giving the benefit of the doubt you have done no harm, and can always avoid any impulsive responses that may later reflect negatively on you;

2.  Be sure to block or put aside all judgments as you consider the positions of others. Regardless of the circumstances surrounding the situation, you must be able to objectively evaluate the merits of the views and suggestions being made;

3.  Never patronize or belittle another person, regardless of your perception of the merit of what she has said or done. Not only will this not help the current situation, it will harm you in the long run. Others will perceive you as pompous and subject to a loss of composure; this not only bodes poorly for your day-to-day interactions with colleagues but destroys your managerial potential in the eyes of others.

Following are some general suggestions to improve upon your overall communication and listening skills:

1.  If you are still in college, take courses or get involved in extra-curricular activities designed to enhance effective communication. The communication sciences department undoubtedly offers courses such as effective writing and public speaking, and may even offer specialized courses aimed specifically at organizational communication and business report writing (such courses may also be available through the business school). Relevant extra-curricular activities might include the debate club and the student newspaper;

2. Participate in corporate educational initiatives designed to enhance communication skills. Such initiatives should not be limited solely to middle managers. Many actuaries dismiss such programs as "soft skill development," and not worth their time, but nothing could be further from the truth;

3. The SOA recently implemented the Decision-Making and Communications Module in response to employer feedback that actuaries lack these skills. This module is required for SOA fellowship and can act as a starting point for refining the ability to more clearly communicate. I find, however, that it is easy to revert to old styles unless what we learn is practiced and reinforced;

4. There is a plethora of books written on effective communication techniques. Among the greatest books ever written on effective communication is Robert Carkhuff's *The Art of Helping*, which, after eight editions, is now called *The Art of Helping in the 21st Century*. This timeless reference introduces all of the fundamentals of interpersonal interaction, and illustrates each with specific examples. Though it is clinician-oriented, the techniques are clearly adaptable to the corporate environment, particularly when difficult discussions become necessary. Additionally, a book that addresses the issue of communication, as well as many other important life skills and values, is *Seven Habits of Highly Effective People*, by Stephen Covey.

## 6.4   LEADERSHIP SKILLS

Actuaries are often promoted to leadership positions because they possess superior technical skills. Technical proficiency itself rarely translates directly into good interpersonal and management capabilities. As an actuary, your technical proficiency will carry you in the beginning stages of your career; down the road, however, you will find that development of leadership skills will be crucial to your continued advancement in any organization.

Under this heading, it is my intention to address two related but distinct types of skills, which, when combined form the foundation of leadership:

1. *Managerial* – The ability to formulate a set of strategic goals and direct others effectively toward the successful completion of those goals. This includes business planning, identification of objectives, efficient resource allocation, time budgeting, and many other competencies. One false but somewhat widely held belief regarding managerial skills is that they only pertain to direct supervision of people;

2. *Interpersonal* – The ability to effectively interact with and influence personnel, senior managers, and external constituencies in a way that is conducive to the execution of the directives required for the attainment of the unit's goals. This includes obtaining "buy-in," establishing and maintaining rapport, motivating employees, equitably evaluating and rewarding performance, anticipating obstacles, negotiating with others, and emotional intelligence.

Managerial skills are therefore intended to represent your ability to logistically and functionally run a unit to meet a set of objectives, as well as to direct large initiatives, even if you do not formally manage people. Interpersonal skills are intended to represent your ability to negotiate the human interactions required to put a plan into action. While this decomposition of leadership skills into the subgroups "managerial" and "interpersonal" is certainly nonscientific, it is nonetheless a useful way of viewing leadership and will be adequate for our purposes here.

Regardless of where you work, a day will come when further career advancement will require the execution of managerial duties, which, in turn, depend on the quality of your people skills. Whether you are a consulting actuary dealing with clients, an insurance actuary managing a line of business, or a government actuary auditing the procedures of large companies, you will need to develop:

1. The ability to conceptualize the goal of your project / department / line / unit / company at both the macro and granular levels;

2. The ability to provide clear and efficient directives to achieve the desired objectives;

3. The ability to obtain "buy-in" for important initiatives from colleagues above, at, and below your level;

4. The ability to establish and maintain good employee morale;

5. The ability to provide constructive feedback and improve employee performance and productivity without insulting employees or damaging relationships;

6. The ability to formulate a business plan that satisfies all stakeholder groups without compromising the integrity of the project;

7. The ability to identify and harness the strengths of others when attacking a project or initiative;

8. The ability to maintain an open and accepting attitude to client feedback, employee concerns, and financial results, all of which might suggest the existence of more appropriate methods of execution.

These abilities are deliberately written to be general, so that they will apply to the wide variety of situations in which you, as an actuary, will be required to demonstrate leadership, management, and interpersonal competencies. Be forewarned – many technical thinkers (i.e., other actuaries) may discuss these ideas and competencies as "soft," and may underestimate the impact of such skills on one's career advancement and the performance of the unit; but these skills are among the most important that you can learn, and are ultimately the skills that will determine where your career may peak.

Though an entire survey of leadership skills and specific examples pertaining to each would be clearly beyond the scope of this book, I am prepared to offer some basic suggestions for developing leadership competencies.

First, for managerial skills:

1. The most straightforward way to acquire managerial skills is to pursue an advanced degree, typically an MBA. Many companies will even provide financial support for such an endeavor. Also, since this provides you with an official credential, it may be particularly useful if you are not currently in a leadership position, but seeking one;

2. Read a few good books. There are probably thousands of books written on managerial skills, approaching the subject from many different angles and referencing many different applications. Some very good titles in this area, which can serve as excellent introductory reading, are:

   a. *The Essential Drucker: The Best of Peter Drucker's Essential Writings on Management*, by Peter Drucker;

   b. *The Fifth Discipline*, by Peter Senge;

   c. *From Engineer to Manager: Mastering the Transition*, by Michael Aucoin.

   Colleagues will undoubtedly be able to recommend some additional titles as well;

3. Many organizations provide training and educational initiatives aimed at emerging leaders. Be sure to take advantage of these opportunities whenever they arise. Your organization may also be willing to send you to a professionally taught management seminar, available from a variety of external providers such as *The Center for Creative Leadership*;

4. Discuss managerial development with co-workers who have succeeded in this regard. You will get valuable advice from people that have conquered the obstacles you are facing;

5. Consult the website of the American Management Association for useful links and ideas, at www.amanet.org.

For interpersonal skills:

1. Literature on interpersonal skills is abundant, and reading a few good titles is definitely a great way to begin. To start, I recommend the following:

    a. *Primal Leadership: Realizing the Power of Emotional Intelligence*, by Daniel Goleman;

    b. *The Handbook of Emotionally Intelligent Leadership; Inspiring Others to Achieve Results*, by Daniel Feldman.

2. Attend any corporate-sponsored programs on giving and accepting feedback, empowering others, and motivational speaking;

3. Know thyself! Most people underestimate the importance of being actively familiar with their own personalities when effectively interacting with others. It is particularly important to work on features of your temperament that may challenge your efficacy, and to be aware of any personal idiosyncrasies that may cause you to exhibit undesirable behaviors when triggered;

4. Know others. Try earnestly to understand different personality styles. This can best be assessed in a group setting with a personality test such as Myers-Briggs. To learn more about Myers-Briggs, consult an HR professional at your company or log on to www.myersbriggs.org.

In addition, an excellent book that encompasses many of the concepts and ideas discussed here is *The Influential Actuary*, by David Miller. In this book, Miller describes skills for interpersonal effectiveness, effective communication, relationships, and moving outside of your comfort zone. I would endorse this book for those aspiring to grow their actuarial careers.

## 6.5    Things to Learn, For Sure

There are many topics one must learn in order to be successful on actuarial exams. There are far fewer topics of which one must indefinitely retain a detailed working knowledge in order to practice successfully as an actuary. This is due to several factors. First, actuarial exams are general in nature while the duties of many actuaries are not. For example, the SOA's Fundamentals of Actuarial Practice course includes an introduction to many areas of current actuarial practice. While I found it interesting at the time, I have never made use of information related to health or property-casualty insurance or defined benefit pension plans as a practicing actuary and doubt that I could do so now without reverting back to the literature. This is not to say, of course, that the information is not useful ... clearly it is; but only that it is not particularly important to me in performing my daily tasks. In addition, many topics covered by textbooks have been made obsolete by advances in technology, or will have been made obsolete in short order. One example I can recall is learning of Newton's method for numerically solving for the internal rate of return of a set of cash flows. Once a very tedious calculation, this can now be done in less than 1 second with generic spreadsheet software by someone with only a rudimentary knowledge of finance.

By and large, the range of topics proving useful to a given actuary in performing day-to-day duties is obviously highly dependent upon that individual's career path. In advance, it may be difficult to identify those that will later be important and those that will not.

The goal of this section is to single out three areas of education which, in my opinion, deserve special emphasis by aspiring actuaries since they apply in fundamental ways to all areas of actuarial practice. It is my opinion that these skill areas are so critical for actuaries' future success that those without them will be at a severe disadvantage relative to colleagues. I am recommending a firm personal commitment by all readers to the mastery of the three topics below, not just to aid in exam success, but to enable one to continue to excel in the workplace.

### 6.5.1 Basic Financial Mathematics

The performance of basic interest, annuity, and discounting calculations is something that everyone takes for granted and which few people can consistently do correctly. I have uncovered countless errors in past work that demonstrate a lack of understanding of compounding frequencies, accrual conventions, the difference between spot and forward rates (and how to calculate one from the other), and the like. In some applications, it may not matter; even when calculations such as these are done incorrectly, it is unlikely to materially affect the end result, and so relaxing precision is probably acceptable. But in many cases, actuaries are producing financial results from models that are intended to cover the next 10 – 80 years of experience, and as such, minor differences in conventions and compounding frequencies can result in large changes in actual financial metrics. It is strongly recommended that students take a particular interest in understanding these principles, ensuring they can be applied correctly, and retaining this knowledge.

### 6.5.2 Computer Programming

Actuaries need not be software engineers. That being said, a basic proficiency in computer programming and in some cases database use/design is important. Ad-hoc models often need to be built to perform isolated analyses. This will, in many cases, need to be done in a package designed for generic applications (e.g., spreadsheet software or mathematical/statistical applications) rather than a commercial application designed specifically for actuarial work. In many cases, doing work efficiently requires a modest level of programming.

A generic example is "scenario analysis," in which the analyst desires to compute the results of a given product or financial endeavor under a large number of "states of the world." Having the ability to write basic code that inputs scenario data, cycles through the scenarios and computes results, and then stores those results in another location for later use is extremely advantageous. Tasks such as these are critical to being a successful analyst, and while conceptually simple, can be difficult to implement without basic programming competencies. You will produce less robust work over a much longer timeframe (both clearly undesirable) without such capabilities. Actuaries need not be computer programming specialists (IT professionals can be called upon for truly industrial quality, homegrown applications) but knowing one reasonably powerful and flexible programming language is highly desirable.

Unfortunately, the actuarial credentialing system does not require candidates to be computer proficient (it lags far behind other competing professions in that regard) and so candidates must rely on themselves to bolster knowledge in this area. College courses, outside instructors, and personal references (e.g. books, CDs, etc) can all be good ways to achieve this knowledge.

### 6.5.3  Simulation

This is one other subject area that I feel is underrepresented in the credentialing curriculum. Students receive a cursory overview of simulation and related methods in the preliminary examinations, but it is insufficient for practice.

P&C actuaries may rely heavily on simulation for product pricing, dynamic financial analysis, and/or economic capital determination. Life insurance actuaries may rely on simulation for product pricing and reserving, liability valuation, and/or economic capital calculations. Investment actuaries may rely on simulation for derivative pricing, economic capital generation, and/or credit risk modeling. Many applications and additional practice areas have gone unnamed. It suffices to say that most areas of actuarial practice now require proficiency in Monte Carlo simulation and related methods. Many products have become too complex to be managed with traditional actuarial methods; expectations and risk metrics can no longer be computed analytically from assumed aggregate loss distributions and other liability characteristics.

Commercial packages may contain embedded simulation modules, and many actuaries may believe that knowledge of how to operate such software will relieve them of the burden of learning about simulation. But "black box" models operated without a fundamental understanding of nested computational methodologies present grave danger. Actuaries who are knowledgeable enough to interpret the output of such models are very valuable to the companies for which they work, and are more likely to translate model outputs into tangible decisions.

## 6.6 CONTINUING EDUCATION

Actuarial science, like most professional disciplines, is dynamic. It changes in response to technological development, globalization, product innovation, legislative initiatives, academic research, and a variety of other factors. It is therefore incumbent upon you, as an actuary, to stay abreast of the latest developments in your area of practice, not only to ensure the utilization of the most appropriate techniques for various applications, but also to enhance your job security.

It is often challenging for actuaries that have practiced for a long time under an existing paradigm to modify their methods to accommodate new advancements. It is often difficult to balance time spent meeting the demands of their jobs with time spent developing aptitude for new techniques. But markets and products are changing very rapidly. Defined benefit pension plans face new challenges, as their popularity diminishes, and employers struggle to fund plans in a low interest rate environment and in the aftermath of one of the worst equity market declines in our nation's history. We struggle to find solutions to our health care crises. The line between insurance and investment products has never been so blurry. Accounting scandals have created a future environment that will undoubtedly demand greater regulatory scrutiny and modified accounting and valuation standards. Insurers face the prospect of new risks, such as bioterrorism, cyberterrorism, and suicide bombings, that have never before been confronted. Without a concerted effort toward learning and implementing new risk management techniques, monitoring evolutions in the business marketplace and global economic environments, identifying and quantifying risks of the 21$^{st}$ century, and making full use of technological advancement, actuaries run the risk of jeopardizing the safety and solvency of their employers, and ultimately, the public confidence.

To ensure appropriate continuing education, I would suggest the following:

1.  Whenever possible, attend seminars geared toward your practice area that are offered by the professional actuarial associations or other organizations whose members have common interests;

2.  Periodically renew your understanding of the "big picture" in your industry / line of business by reading the newspaper, subscribing to journals and magazines, speaking with other professionals in the field, and monitoring the activities of competitors;

3.  Attend a SOA/CAS/CIA meeting at least once every two years. In addition to the break-out sessions, the networking opportunities are extremely valuable. If you are unable to attend, browse the program and order recordings for those sessions that might promote your continuing education;

4.  Monitor actuarial publications to keep up with new research and emerging areas of interest.

5.  Periodically search for textbooks that address emerging topics.

In recognition of the important role of continuing education, the SOA has a Continuing Professional Development (**CPD**) requirement, which applies to all of its members. While you will have the opportunity to become thoroughly familiar with this requirement after attaining membership, it is primarily aimed at ensuring that members' knowledge is continually enhanced in view of emerging developments. It is an "honors system" approach in which members personally attest to their own satisfaction of the requirements, but is subject to random and occasion audit by the SOA. More information can be found on the SOA website. All other actuarial organizations have a similar requirement.

## 6.7    BUSINESS ACUMEN

The term **business acumen** refers to an individual's ability to fully comprehend all aspects of the business environment in which she works, and to successfully integrate all considerations (many of them conflicting) when making business decisions or providing feedback to the decision-maker(s). Though each of the previous sections in this chapter have hinted at this theme in some way, it is critical to recognize business acumen as a standalone competency.

Actuaries are forced to balance the development of a very specialized analytical skill set with the acquirement of "big picture" organizational knowledge. The focused modeling work that actuaries perform exacerbates this challenge, since it often requires that significant portions of time be spent constructing and fine-tuning models. While this function is absolutely mission-critical to any organization engaged in the business of managing financial risk, its highly specialized focus can sometimes have the unfortunate consequence of limiting actuaries' exposure to important functions performed by other areas of the company. This is particularly true for actuaries in the beginning stages of their careers.

Thus, due to the concentrated nature of their duties, actuaries are sometimes unable to fully grasp all of the issues associated with the organization's multiple constituencies, a dynamic which has the potential to create significant problems when many areas of the company are called upon to work together.

The development of business acumen is both an active and passive endeavor. Here are some suggestions for actively developing your own business acumen:

1.  During each project, be sure to ask your supervisor or other involved employees about the big picture. Be sure you understand the end goal, the role of each intermediary, and how your duties contribute to the success of the project;

2. Gain a thorough understanding of your company, including each of its lines of business, its different product suites, and its major distribution channels. This can be accomplished by networking with actuaries and other individuals in the company, reading company literature, attending company functions, and participating in formal corporate programs aimed at development of employee awareness;

3. Take advantage of all opportunities to interact with individuals outside of your area. This may include meetings with producers, underwriters, external constituencies, marketing staff, account-ants, and others.

For actuaries, business acumen takes many forms. Chiefly, however, it includes the ability to:

1. Objectively consider the situation from all angles prior to responding, when asked to make business decisions that will re-duce profitability or increase risk. This includes an analysis of sales levels and pressure, the unit's profitability and growth tar-gets, the current state of the market, any potential ethical conse-quences, and a variety of other factors that are situation-specific;

2. Understand that short- and long-term accounting consequences may restrict raw economic flexibility;

3. Understand that product innovation is meaningless if the end result is a lack of marketability;

4. Understand that mathematical models are at best imperfect representations of reality, and not the solution to every business problem. Emanuel Derman and Paul Wilmott have written an excellent document on this topic called the "Financial Modelers' Manifesto" which interested readers can find on the internet.

## 6.8   CONCLUSION

Each of the skill areas discussed in this chapter is fundamentally important to a successful career in business. I encourage you to pursue additional education in each of these areas; you will be well served by them both in a professional and personal sense. While I have provided some advice on basic fundamentals, each of these concepts is a large discipline with many other insights to share, so be generous with your time.

The completion of your actuarial exams is not the end of your education, for a successful actuarial career requires life-long learning. But you need not worry; you'll enjoy the ride. So says the *Jobs Rated Almanac*!

# INDEX

SOA (see Society of Actuaries)
SOA.org   23, 32
Society of Actuaries   11-12, 17-24
Society of Pension Actuaries   14
Study Manuals   38-39, 72-73, 84-85
Study schedule   74-76
Superstition   93-96
Syllabus of Basic Education   28

Tax-Exempt and Governmental Plan
    Consultant   14
TGPC (see Tax-Exempt and
    Governmental Plan Consultant)
Time Management   44, 76
True/False   52

UAP (see University Accreditation
    Program)
University Accreditation Program   30

Validation by Educational Experience
    18, 19, 20, 27
VEE (see Validation by Educational
    Experience)